WELCOMING RESPONSIBILITIES

30 Ways for Older Teens and Young Adults to Handle Responsibilities

ISRAELIN SHOCKNESS

Successful Youth Living - Vol. 2

Vanquest Publishing Inc.

Requests for information can be obtained by contacting info@IsraelinShockness.com

VAN QUEST PUBLISHING
motivating | inspiring | educating

Cataloguing-in-Publication Data

Israelin Shockness

Includes bibliographical references

WELCOMING RESPONSIBILITIES

30 Ways for Older Teens and Young Adults to Handle Responsibilities

ISBN: 978-1775009443 (Paperback)

ISBN: 978-0-9940486-9-1 (Ebook)

SERIES- Successful Youth Living - Vol. 2

DISCLAIMER

All materials provided in this book are for informational purposes only and should not be taken as a substitute for professional, psychological, or mental health advice. These materials are intended to encourage and motivate readers to think and to have meaningful conversations around the issues discussed, the objective being to promote more responsible behavior at all times. If, for any reason, a reader may be experiencing any emotional or other crisis, that reader is encouraged to seek out professional care. References have been made to peer-reviewed and other research studies and works, but this is not intended to imply specific endorsement of this author's work by any of these authors and professionals mentioned. Any incorrect attribution of ideas to an author was not intentional and will be corrected at earliest possibility. The opinions expressed in this book are solely those of this author and not those of the publisher. Further, the publisher is exempt from any responsibility for actions taken by readers with respect to the content. The publisher also acknowledges that readers act of their own accord in using information presented and hold the author and the publisher blameless in the readers' use of the content.

PURPOSE OF THIS SERIES

Successful Youth Living is a series of books, dealing with issues, which older teens and young adults face as they go through the uncertainty of adolescence. A few of the topics dealt with are: becoming a leader in your own right without being a bully; learning how to assume responsibility; fostering positive attitudes and habits for self-growth; learning how to continue your education regardless of where you stopped or whether you dropped out; developing emotional intelligence and caring for self and others; learning how to deal with stress; recognizing the importance of personal reflection; and being a person that others admire for the right reasons.

The 'seed' for these volumes was actually planted when the author, then a teenager on a scholarship, almost dropped out of university because of her inability to deal with many issues that had nothing to do with school. Thanks to the insightfulness and mentorship of a professor, the author became a teen mentor and since then have committed herself to paying it forward by looking out for vulnerable teens and young adults that have lost their way, the way she had almost lost hers. After years of further study, a career as an educator working with children, teens and young adults, years as a volunteer in marginalized communities and as a columnist in a weekly community newspaper, Israelin has recognized that many of the issues plaguing adolescents have not changed. She has therefore decided to share ideas she has gleaned from personal experience, as well as from her students, readers, studies, and from peer-reviewed articles.

The hope is that these ideas would be a catalyst for thinking and discussion among teens and young adults, preparing them for making split-minute decisions that they may face in the future.

DEDICATION

I dedicate this book to teens and young adults and to the older adults who care about them. Going through the transitional stage of adolescence can be very challenging and sometimes confusing to young people. Not only is this a period of many physical changes, but it is also a period of emotional, intellectual, cognitive, and social changes. Some young people take the position that no one really understands them. Many in this group sometimes become despondent, seeing life as having little or no meaning. However, there are many adolescents who are well organized and adjusted and who live balanced lives. Many of these reach out and lend a helping hand to their less-adjusted peers and friends.

Whether part of Generation X, Generation Y/Millennial, or Generation Z, some young people face perennial issues that are part of growing up. Although the generations may have different ways of looking at issues, the fact remains that similar problems and challenges still persist. And even as some Generation Z individuals are becoming parents to Generation Alpha children, they are finding that these challenges are becoming even more complex.

A major challenge that many young people have to grapple with is that of taking responsibility, with some thinking that they need not even consider doing so as they are still very young. But this way of thinking could lead to utter confusion, when some young people, not being prepared for handling certain responsibilities, are forced to face stark reality.

They may find that they need to act, but not having even considered the possibility of certain issues and the responsibilities involved, they must make what could be life-changing decisions on the spot. This could be a very daunting task for even the bravest. With the age of youth extending from the teenage years well into their thirties, many young people are now facing challenges as to when to take on adult roles and how to go about doing so. This "trying on" of adult roles is individual and unique and presents many challenges to these young people in this liminal state of adolescence.

The truth is, responsibility is part of life and the earlier young people consider various issues that are part of life and learn to be responsible, the easier life tends to become. Considering some of the ways that young people see and deal with responsibility is an important part of learning how to eventually become full-fledged responsible adults.

The issues and ideas expressed in this book could therefore be used for self-reflection or for group discussion.

To Young People:

If you are a teen or young adult, I encourage you, after reading this book and maybe after implementing some of the strategies mentioned, to share some of these ideas with friends, family members, and peers. Also, think of ways that you may use this information and any motivational statements in your personal life.

To Adults:

If you are a teacher, group leader, or other adult who work with young people, think of ways that this information and any motivational statements could be used to stimulate discussion within your class or group. If you are a parent, think of the ways you can use these and other ideas to help the young people you love, children and stepchildren, become more responsible and caring individuals.

To All:

Fireside or online chats, dinner conversations, recess chatter, watercooler talk, and classroom discussions are all opportunities for sharing. The opening to these talks could be simply, "I was reading a book today and it got me thinking about ___. What do you think?" One thing may lead to another and before you know it, you can be having a vibrant conversation on the subject of how to promote responsibilities among young people. You may find that introducing a subject could lead to the opening up of channels for better communication with some young people who may be suffering in silence.

I would welcome hearing about your experiences and would appreciate your feedback, which I would use to improve on this book. I can be reached at info@SuccessfulYouthLiving.com.

Also, remember to share your positive comments as online reviews wherever you obtained this book. Thanks.

TABLE OF CONTENTS

CHAPTER 1

TAKING RESPONSIBILITY FOR YOURSELF

Frustration, anger and violence are often associated. When individuals strive to achieve a goal, they sometimes encounter barriers and this could lead to frustration and stress. At times, frustration and stress could lead to anger, and when some individuals become angry they may also become violent.

UNDERLYING FACTORS

As one source points out, the reason that individuals often experience anger and frustration stems from the fact that they have certain expectations of how things should be (Vilhauer, April 19, 2015). When individuals confront situations where things are not going according to expectations, they become frustrated. These expectations are usually based on individuals having something like a 'personal rulebook' that says how things should go and that "incorporates . . . (their) beliefs, perspectives, likes, ideals, and values" (Vilhauer, April 19, 2015). The frustration and anger individuals experience often stem from the fact that they perceive others as not playing by their rules.

RELATIONSHIP BETWEEN FRUSTRATION AND STRESS

When individuals become frustrated, this becomes part of what contributes to stress. Stress is really the building up of emotions such as frustration, anger, aggressiveness, anxiety, despair and a host of negative emotions. When individuals experience stress, some are prone to become violent. Stress can be seen to be closely related to frustration. When individuals believe that the rules by which they live their lives and by which they expect society to work are being violated or eroded, they may become frustrated. When they believe that there is not much they can do to change things, they become even more frustrated. Frustration is therefore also seen as stemming from stress (Kane, October 8, 2018).

WHY FRUSTRATION AND STRESS CAN BE DANGEROUS

The danger stems from the fact that if individuals are continually feeling frustrated and experience stress, these experiences could have a negative effect on their bodies. According to Kane (October 8, 2018),

"Repeated stress that is not effectively dealt with can cause serious physical consequences. Like a machine that eventually wears down, continued stressors on the body's activation of the nervous system (chronic stress) results in release of the stress hormones of cortisol and epinephrine and precipitates problems with the heart and other vital organs, along with the potential development of mental health issues".

In light of the effects that stress can have on the human body, individuals are encouraged to look for ways of identifying, precipitating and addressing the issues that cause stress. It is important to look out for signs that one is frustrated and under stress and consider ways of dealing with these negative emotions.

WAYS TO IDENTIFY FRUSTRATION AND STRESS

It is important that individuals know how to identify their frustration and stress, because they would then be in a better position to deal with them more effectively.

WATCH FOR IMPULSIVE ACTION

Common sense thinking tells us that when individuals are used to doing things easily, when confronted with barriers in achieving their goals, they could become very frustrated. They could also become impulsive and take hasty action to find a solution. Impulsive action, or action that is not thoroughly thought out, could sometimes result in violent and unintended consequences.

CLEAR THINKING NECESSARY

Therefore, the counsel is to take time to think before making decisions. Individuals who make hasty decisions often fail to take all aspects of a situation into consideration. In some instances, these individuals may become so overwhelmed with anger and other emotions that they are unable to think clearly. By being conscious of needing to think clearly can help the situation.

WAYS TO DEAL WITH FRUSTRATION AND STRESS

Some of the suggested ways to deal with frustration and stress are discussed below.

TAKE SOME TIME OUT

If you feel that you are in a constant state of stress and you are feeling overwhelmed, take some time out. Take some deep breaths and this will very likely help to calm you down. This will come about because when you are frustrated or under stress, you tend to take shallow breaths, which means that your body is not getting sufficient oxygen. When you stop and breathe deeply, this will help to replenish some of the oxygen you so desperately need.

IDENTIFY THE SOURCE OF YOUR FRUSTRATION

By taking some time out and thinking about the source of your frustration, you are very likely going to be able to identify what is bothering you so much. It is also likely that in doing so, you would find out what an underlying problem is. In this state of contemplation, you may have some constructive ideas about how to deal with the problem that is causing you so much stress.

CONTEMPLATE SCENARIOS AHEAD OF TIME

You may have figured out what causes you so much frustration. One way of dealing with this frustration is to try to develop some resilience. In other words, think of other ways of looking at the situation that caused you frustration. As one source points out, "change how you perceive frustration and stress" (Kane, October 8, 2018).

Rather than become annoyed that something does not go the way you expect it to go, change your expectation and reaction so that the whole experience is not so frustrating. Considering issues ahead of time can provide you with the opportunities to contemplate scenarios that you may face in the future. Having considered difficult issues and contemplated possible scenarios, you may be better prepared to deal with the real life challenges, when they appear.

PREPARATION REDUCES FRUSTRATION

With preparation, frustration could be reduced, as alternatives may have been considered with preparation. Anger and hasty action are also reduced, which could prevent or minimize violence. Therefore, by considering what you may do if confronted with a challenge, you are preparing yourself to be able to cope with the challenge more successfully. Preparation can include discussion and in having others with whom to exchange ideas.

Chapter 1 - Food For Thought

Topics and Ideas for Self-Reflection and Discussion

Self-Reflection:

How do I deal with frustration and stress? If I wanted to improve how I cope with stress and frustration, what are some of the things I would?

Group Discussion

How can I share this idea with family members and class mates?

I can start a fireside chat or an online group with friends ___

I can discuss with family members at dinner _____

I can do a class presentation on coping with stress _____

I can have coffee with a friend _____

Other ideas and topics for discussion _____

CHAPTER 1 - REFERENCES AND FURTHER READING

American Association of Child and Adolescent Psychiatry (2014). Helping teenagers with stress.

http://www.aacap.org/AACAP/Families_and_Youth/Facts _for_Families/Facts_for_families_Pages/Helping_ Teenagers_With_Stress_66.aspx

Jakobsson, A. (2006). Students' self-confidence and learning through dialogues in a Net-based environment. Journal of Technology and Teacher Education, 14(2), 387-405

Kane, S. (October 8, 2018). My Best Ways to Deal with Frustration.

PsychCentral. Available at https://psychcentral.com/lib/my-best-ways-to-deal-with-frustration/

Schwartz-Mette, R. a. & Rose, A. J. (2009). Conversational self-focus in adolescent friendships: Observational assessment of an interpersonal process and relations with internalizing symptoms and friendship quality. Journal of social and Clinical Psychology, 28(10), 1263-1297.

Singh, A. (July 3, 2017). How to Control Anger and Frustration. Your Health Support. Available at https://www.yourhealthsupport.in/how-to-control-anger-and-frustration/

Vilhauer, J. (April 19, 2015). 3 Simple Steps to Control Anger and Frustration with Others. Available at https://www.psychologytoday.com/us/blog/living-forward/201504/3-simple-steps-control-anger-and-frustration-others

TAKING RESPONSIBILITY FOR YOUR ACTIONS

Although this may appear to be a very obvious statement, many individuals have difficulty taking responsibility for their actions. Many people explain that the reason that they may have done something was because of their circumstances. Probably poor home life made it difficult for them to resist the temptation to steal. They argue, if only they had enough to begin with, they would not have succumbed to the temptation. They may argue that the reason that they got into a fight was because someone called them a bad name, and they had to respond. Some people make bad decisions at work, and instead of acknowledging that they made a mistake, they try to blame someone else for it.

DON'T PLAY THE BLAME GAME

The truth is, there are many circumstances in life that could lead people to make mistakes and take undesirable action having poor results. Rather than play the blame game and try to implicate someone else for your actions and decision-making, take responsibility for your actions, regardless of how wrong-headed those actions may be.

You Will Be a Better Person

What does this achieve? It allows you to come face to face with the mistakes that you have made, and having accepted and owned them, you will learn from them. If you keep blaming others and never take responsibility for your mistakes, you would have convinced yourself that you are never wrong. This means that you would never be in a position to correct your mistakes.

Your Self-Respect Will Grow

Worse than that, you would alienate others around you, because they would realize that you cannot take responsibility for your actions. Start acknowledging your mistakes and see your self-respect grow.

Identifying Problem Areas

How can you start taking responsibility for your actions? Identify problem areas. Maybe you seem to be encountering difficulty wherever you go, and it appears that people in various areas of your life are picking on you. You may not have had the best circumstances in your early life. You may not be having an easy time at school, or even the best breaks at work. Maybe you are getting into conflict with your parents, siblings, friends, and/or coworkers. You are not sure why you are having so many social conflicts. You reason that you may be picked upon because you are of a different race, ethnicity, language group, or religion, but you are not sure.

REFLECT ON YOUR ACTIONS

The secret to getting to the real reason for your social conflicts is to reflect on your actions. Ask yourself what it is that causes the difficulties you encounter in dealing with people in different areas of your life. Think honestly about the situations and encounters. Think of how you interact with others. Do you project an aggressive personality? Are you argumentative when there is really no need to be? Do people see you in a negative way? Is there something that you are doing that is causing such reaction to you? Are you always shifting the blame, and not taking responsibility? Are you a stand-up guy or gal?

DON'T BE AFRAID TO HAVE A CONVERSATION

Communication is very healthy. Ask a friend or a close acquaintance to be perfectly honest with you. Ask someone who would not be afraid to tell you the truth. If you choose someone who will tell you what you want to hear, you would have sabotaged this exercise. When you ask a question, make it an honest question. Don't frame your question in a way that shows that you expect a particular answer. Be gracious when accepting the answer.

From the honest answer of a friend or acquaintance, you may find out that you instinctively try to give a good impression of yourself by shifting blame to others, and by not sharing in responsibility when something goes wrong and when you are largely to blame. You may be trying too hard to give a good impression of yourself.

ACKNOWLEDGE YOUR ERRORS

If you realize after reflection and conversation that your major fault is not taking responsibility for your actions, you need to acknowledge this and change your approach. Don't be afraid to start taking responsibility for your actions. Let others see the change in you. You may even find that in some cases making apologies for past behavior can be useful. This is not a weakness, but rather a strength. You will be respected for acknowledging your mistakes and trying to improve your actions. You may find that the difficulties you encountered earlier disappear or at least diminish, because you are willing to reflect on your actions and change your ways.

CHAPTER 2- FOOD FOR THOUGHT

TOPICS AND IDEAS FOR SELF-REFLECTION AND DISCUSSION

Self Reflection

"When you keep blaming others for every mistake you make in life, one day you'll look back and realize you're the mistake all along."

— Abdulazeez Henry Musa

"If you feel the need to make someone feel less assured of themselves or have to call another person out, you may gain a false sense of superiority."

—Kristin Michelle Elizabeth

Group Discussion

"All blame is a waste of time. No matter how much fault you find with another, and regardless of how much you blame him, it will not change you. The only thing blame does is to keep the focus off you when you are looking for external reasons to explain your unhappiness or frustration. You may succeed in making another feel guilty about something by blaming him, but you won't succeed in changing whatever it is about you that is making you unhappy." - Wayne Dyer

CHAPTER 2 - REFERENCES AND FURTHER READING

Fast, N. J. (May 13, 2010). How to stop the blame game. Harvard Business Review. Available at https://hbr.org/2010/05/how-to-stop-the-blame-game

Stemke, C. (n.d.) How to take responsibility for your actions. Our Everyday Life. Available at https://oureverydaylife.com/responsibility-actions-4802685.html

CREATING A CIRCLE OF CARING:

BEING OUR BROTHER'S OR SISTER'S KEEPER

Living in a large city in a large industrialized country, we are faced with the phenomenon of large crowds at practically every turn. There are people everywhere, and yet we could feel alone and vulnerable in these crowds. Living in a rural area, although often different in that there are not the major crowds encountered in the large cities, but where there may be opportunity for more intimate relations, we could still feel alone and vulnerable. The reason for this is that we are individuals going about our business, caring for ourselves and often without regard for others around us. Or we may care a great deal for the others around us, but we do not share our most intimate feelings with them. Or we do not show them that we care for them, as much as we actually do.

DISPLAY MORE CARING

We have been conditioned to think that our concern should be only ourselves and those close to us. We often think that other young people – our family members and friends – are capable of taking care of themselves. Consequently, we do not display as much caring for them as we could. We see them as individuals, who are also preoccupied with themselves – and maybe they are.

BECOMING EASY TARGETS

However, by taking the approach of caring for ourselves and without much regard for others, we become easy targets for predators that would prey on young people, on children, and even on some adults. At these times, we wish someone would be aware of the danger and intervene on behalf of those of us at risk.

NEED FOR A CARING ENVIRONMENT

The truth is, if we do not have a caring environment, we would not be equipped to recognize when others are in danger, and others would not be able to recognize when we have an urgent need. It is only with caring that we could intuitively tell that a young person walking down the street is in danger and we can intervene on that person's behalf; or that the man or woman standing at the corner of the street needs immediate medical attention to save his or her life, and that we are the only ones present that could get that life-saving attention to this person.

Caring means looking out for others when they are not in a position to look out for themselves, or when they are unaware of impending danger.

CHANGING SELF-CENTEREDNESS TO CIRCLE OF CARING

To change the self-centeredness in our society, we have to start with ourselves. If we could care about others, maybe they too would learn to care about others, and in time the circle of caring could become larger. We could become a caring society. This may appear as a pipe dream, but it isn't.

It would take time for our circle of caring to spread, for as the saying goes, "Rome was not built in a day." If we start with ourselves, chances are we would influence those around us to be caring about others.

DON'T LOSE HOPE IF YOU CARE

There are already individuals among us who care for others, and who may find that others do not reciprocate and do not share the same caring attitude towards them or others. In some cases, those individuals who show caring to others may not be appreciated and may even be seen as 'different' or as wanting something from the people for whom they care. Caring could sometimes be mistaken for need. But a word to those who care. Don't lose heart, for an act of caring can motivate another person to show caring to still yet another person. And the circle can continue.

WE DON'T NEED DISASTER

We do not have to wait until disaster strikes in order to show our caring. We need to do so under normal everyday circumstances, for it is by caring that we would eliminate some of the atrocious things that take place in our society.

BE YOUR SISTER'S OR BROTHER'S KEEPER

We can start by being our brother's and sister's keeper. We can do this in several ways. We can literally help our brother or sister avoid danger, and we can also prevent our brother or sister from being a danger to self as well as to others. We have a responsibility to do so for the good of all people, including our family members. This also holds true for friends. This is particularly the case if we know that a family member has a problem that needs monitoring.

It then becomes our responsibility to do something to minimize danger that that family member poses to himself, herself or to others. We are not showing love to our family member or concern to society by hiding the fact that our family member is an imminent threat. It is love and concern that would guide us to take whatever action is necessary to prevent harm.

HELP AVOID DANGER

We are our brother's and sister's keeper in helping him or her avoid danger. Sometimes young people do not see the potential danger in the things they do, and adults could draw their attention to these. Sometimes children may do things that could cause them physical harm, and we could help to guide them away from danger to some more appropriate activity. In so doing, we could explain the potential danger so that children would avoid these dangers in the future. With young people, it may not be as easy to guide them to take different action. For example, we may accompany a friend who decides to take a walk by herself or himself, and we can be simply a buddy. The buddy system has been known to work well as a safety strategy. Another example is where we may talk to a family member or friend whom we know is troubled, or where we may simply keep that person company when we know he or she really doesn't want to be alone or shouldn't be. We may also help that young person to think more clearly and rationally by being a good listener.

BE SUPPORTIVE OF FAMILY MEMBERS

We are our brother's and sister's keeper by preventing our family member from posing danger to himself, herself or others. Most of us live in families and through our interaction with family members often know when things are going well or badly for them. We could often tell if they feel overwhelmed, and we often know their health history. With the vast amount of stress in our society today, mental illness in its many forms has become very commonplace. We have to be supportive of our family members. We have a similar responsibility to close friends, many of whom may confide their problems in us.

CARING FOR MENTALLY ILL FAMILY MEMBERS OR FRIENDS

When a family member is diagnosed with some form of mental illness, it is our responsibility to ensure that the family member receives the appropriate care. This means seeing to it that the family member is taking his or her medication correctly, that his or her condition is not deteriorating, and that he or she is functioning adequately. If we have any concern that this is not happening, then we need to be responsible enough to help our family member. Failing this, we could be exposing our family member to harm from himself or herself, and we can put the family and the community at risk. This fact cannot be stressed too strongly.

No Regrets

How many times have we heard commented that a young person who may have committed an atrocious act was mentally ill! How many times have we heard family members comment that they thought everything was fine, although the person withdrew from contact!

The question then becomes, if the person withdrew and did not want contact, what are we then to do? We have to be guided by compassion, by empathy, and by understanding. We have to question ourselves whether that person is in a safe place, or capable of acting irrationally. At times, we have heard comments about a person "spiraling down" where some intervention may have helped. Intervention could be as little as talking to our family member or friend. This is a difficult call, but thinking of the possible consequences of doing nothing is usually a good place to start.

Do Something

If we know or believe our family member or friend is about to do something terrible and irrational, it becomes our responsibility to do something to stop him or her. If our family member or friend may have jokingly suggested that he or she would commit a serious act, it is our responsibility to take action to prevent such an action from taking place.

YOU MAY BE THE ONLY ONE

If, as a young person, you are aware that a friend or family member has become involved in drug use, or you suspect that person is experimenting with drugs, you may be the only person that could influence your family member or friend to stop using, or the only person that could show that young person the folly of his or her ways.

WE CARE WHEN WE ARE OUR BROTHER'S OR SISTER'S KEEPER

By being our brother's and sister's keeper, we take the time to care about others. This circle of caring could expand to include people who are not related, and who are not friends. What we dream about is a caring society, where people are safe because they care about others and they know others care about them. Even when there are predators around, people should feel confident that in difficult situations, they could count on help.

LET'S NOT WAIT FOR DISASTERS

Are you your brother's or sister's keeper? You may find that caring for your family member or friend is only the beginning of caring for others. When you care for others, others are likely to care for you. Often in a time of extreme crisis, like when a tornado hits an area, we hear of strangers coming together to help each other. Imagine what it would be like if we did not wait for disasters in order to make us not only care, but show caring to others. Think of the small caring things you can do today, like caring about how your family member or your friend feels, that can usher in a circle of caring.

CHAPTER 3 - FOOD FOR THOUGHT

TOPICS AND IDEAS FOR SELF-REFLECTION AND DISCUSSION

Self-Reflection

Can I describe myself as a caring person?

What caring things do I do?

How can I make myself more caring?

Do I have plans to be a more caring person?

What are those plans?

Group Discussion

What is the significance of these sayings?

"Even the smallest act of caring for another person is like a drop of water – it will make ripples throughout the entire pond." – Jessy and Bryan Matteo

"Friendly people are caring people, eager to provide encouragement and support when needed most." – Rosabeth Moss Kanter

"Try to be a rainbow in someone else's cloud." – Maya Angelou

TAKING RESPONSIBILITY FOR ADDRESSING BULLYING

Bullying is a serious problem that causes much hurt to individuals, much of this lasting a lifetime. Part of taking responsibility for oneself must involve preventing bullies from taking advantage against oneself and others. Young people are often ostracized and excluded, if they do not conform. Not dressing like others, not doing the same things, and often appearing different would quickly draw the attention of others. Therefore, the fear of being ostracized or of being excluded is a real fear that leads many young people to behave like others, and to get caught up in activities that they would not otherwise entertain. Many parents would swear that their young people would definitely not be involved in certain activities, only to discover later that they were wrong. Part of the reason for this is that many parents believe that they know their young people's character very well, but they fail to recognize their young people's actions and motivations in a group setting. Many young people, faced with bullying or the prospect of such action, behave very differently from how they would behave under normal conditions.

BULLYING IS PREVALENT

Bullying is a practice that is commonplace. In more recent times, some people see bullying as a sign of strength. Although people pay lip-service to the idea that bullying should not be tolerated, in their everyday lives they model bullying for younger people.

We see it among siblings, among children on the playground, among employees in the workplace, and even among politicians seeking coveted positions. The general approach seems to be to target those that appear weak or different. But let's look at bullying from the perspective of the young person.

WHO ARE THE BULLIES?

Who are the bullies? Bullies could be young people or adults. According to the profiles provided by some social psychologists and psychiatrists, school bullies could be relatively shy individuals who find their strength in taking advantage of others, usually others smaller than they are. These shy and socially isolated individuals may find that they have friends when they join in to take advantage of another young person. Some young people are so insecure that they believe picking on someone else would prevent others from picking on them. Various studies have revealed bullies to be of various subtypes (Espelage, 2001; Piotrowski & Hoot, 2008; Peeters, Cillessen, & Scholte, 2010).

BULLIES OFTEN SEE THEMSELVES AS BETTER

Bullies are also seen as individuals that hold contempt, disdain and dislike for others, that see themselves as better than those they bully. They believe they are better because they see those they bully as different and inferior. The difference bullies see could be based on race, religion, physical appearance, being new at a school, or any other feature that they identify as making the other person inferior to them.

SUBTYPES OF BULLIES

Bullies are seen as a heterogeneous group and their behaviors vary among adolescents. In fact, according to one study, "changes and transitions during adolescence are associated with bullying behavior and provisions of bullying behavior" (Peeters et al., 2010, p. 1050). These researchers also identified three subtypes of adolescent bullies, namely, a popular-socially intelligent group, a popular moderate group, and an unpopular-less-socially intelligent group (Peeters et al., 2010). These subtypes differ depending on the function that the bullying serves.

BULLIES OFTEN HAVE PROBLEMS

Bullies may be young people with their own emotional problems who find escape in bullying. Some bullies are young people who are bullied at home. They may be the victims of abuse in their own homes and may find an outlet for their hostilities outside the home. They may take out their anger and frustration on others. The typical bully is not a large individual who is an outcast, but rather someone popular, usually a male. Studies have also shown that bullies are both male and female, usually popular people who target others who are usually not popular and who may appear 'different' (Peeters et al., 2010).

SOME BULLIES HAVE BEEN BULLIED

According to a more common theory of bullying, bullies are people who were once bullied or who are still being bullied in a particular setting In this situation, the bullying may be seen as resulting from anger. It has been noted that bullies that have been bullied are often more aggressive than those bullies that have not been bullied.

BULLYING AS UNINHIBITED BEHAVIOR

Social psychologists tell us that when people are in a crowd, they are often uninhibited and may do things that they would not normally do when they are alone. In two recent instances of bullying, one in western Canada and the other in the United States, some young bullies led to the deaths of their victims. In the Canadian case, a group of young people teased, taunted, and then drowned the young girl they were teasing. In the American case, a group of girls and boys hanged the girl they were teasing. These are extreme cases of murder, showing the extent to which bullying could lead to despicable and otherwise uninhibited actions on the part of young people acting in groups.

HERE COME THE BYSTANDERS

Apart from the bullies and the bullied, there are the bystanders. The bystanders are all others who look on or look the other way, or downplay the interaction, when bullies target children or young people. Some bystanders may cheer the bully on because they want to be friends with the bully, whom they perceive as being popular. Other bystanders tell themselves that what is going on is none of their business and so try to ignore it.

Others, usually adults, discount the interaction, honestly believing that what they are seeing are young people teasing each other in fun. They overlook the fact that the person who is being teased really does not appreciate the teasing and wants it stopped. Others take the position that the bullied person must have asked for it. There may also be other bystanders who want to do something but who are afraid that they may become the next target, if they tried to intervene.

BULLYING ACTIONS

Bullying actions may involve teasing others at school and making them uncomfortable even when they show their displeasure at the teasing. Laughing at others or causing them to feel isolated or inferior is another form of bullying. Physically beating up on others or threatening to do so and intimidating others by words or actions are all examples of bullying.

EFFECTS OF BULLYING ON OTHERS

Think of the effects these actions may be having on the other young people that are bullied! While these bullying actions may appear harmless to some bullies that rationalize their behavior as "joking around", these actions may be having a terrible impact. These actions may be physical but can leave deep emotional scars for decades on those that are being bullied. Bullying is violence.

RETALIATION WITH VIOLENCE

Young people who feel helpless in bullying situations may be bullied for some time. Then there comes a time when they may decide that they have had enough – as much as they would take. This could be catastrophic. In recent months and years, school violence has escalated, and it has been attributed to young people who have been bullied and have eventually retaliated with violence. While this is no excuse for those young people to take the lives of others, these incidents just throw light on the extent of the emotional chaos that could be caused by bullying.

DON'T BE INTIMIDATED

If you are being bullied, you should not feel too intimidated to do something about it. Regardless of your age, you should report any bullying to your parents, your teacher, your principal, or even to the police, especially if there is a threat on your life or on the lives of family members.

Bullying is a serious matter and should be treated as such. You ought to seek help as soon as the bullying begins. Reporting it to a proper authority is important. Don't be afraid to take action early. Waiting only intensifies the situation and can cause greater emotional harm. Remember, bullies are most likely insecure cowards who are afraid to be themselves, or who depend on their teasing and bullying to appear popular.

YOUR RESPONSIBILITY TO REPORT BULLYING

If you are a bystander, a young person who sees bullying taking place, it is your responsibility to report it. The person who is being bullied may be too intimidated to do anything about it, even though that person may be hurting very badly. It is true that a young person may perceive a bullying situation as potentially dangerous and may not want to intervene. This does not mean that the bystander should keep quiet for fear of being targeted. That young person should seek immediate help, particularly if the potential exists for the situation to escalate into something more serious. It may be prudent to inform school officials if the bullying takes place on school grounds. In other situations, it may be best to call police.

MAKING THE DECISION TO SPEAK UP ABOUT BULLYING

Therefore, if you are being bullied, make a decision to speak up about the bully and tell someone who can do something about your bullying experience. For example, if the bullying takes place at school, speak to your teacher or the principal about it. Also, tell your parents. If the matter is unmanageable and takes place outside of school, ask your parents to report it to law enforcement. It makes no sense to suffer in silence, because the bullying would continue.

MAKING THE DECISION TO STOP BULLYING

If you are a bully, it is high time you stop bullying. Some believe that those who bully are really cowards who feel insecure. This may be the time for you to seek out some help for your insecurity and your bullying. How would you feel being in the situation where you cause emotional distress to others, which could last a lifetime for the persons being bullied? How would you feel if you were the one experiencing this bullying? Put yourself in the place of the person you victimized with bullying.

MAKING THE DECISION TO SPEAK OUT AGAINST BULLYING

If you are a bystander and see bullying taking place, it is time you muster up enough courage to speak out against this situation. How would you feel knowing that you neglected to take steps that could have ended the suffering that another person was needlessly going through? Bullying is violence that should never be allowed to take place.

CHAPTER 4 - FOOD FOR THOUGHT

TOPICS AND IDEAS FOR SELF-REFLECTION AND
DISCUSSION

Self-Reflection

Thinking of situations when I was bullied, how did that make me feel?

Thinking of situations where I bullied someone, how did that make me feel?

As you look back, how do you feel about laughing at a post someone made about one of my classmates?

How do I think the person who was cyberbullied felt?

What would I do differently, if I am faced a similar situations again?

Group Discussion:

What could a class or group do to deal with one of its members who is a bully?

What are some strategies that a group can use, if it recognizes that someone is being bullied?

How can a group or class organize a program to promote an anti-bullying? What would the program look like?

CHAPTER 4 - REFERENCES AND FURTHER READING

Arseneault, L., Bowes, L. & Shakoor, S. (2010). Bullying victimization in youths and mental health problems: 'Much ado about nothing?' Psychological Medicine, 40, 717-729

Espelage, D. (2002). Schoolroom Torment: Bullies often try to charm adults, but the pain they cause needs serious attention," People Weekly, February 5.

Munoz, L. C., Qualter, P. & Padgett, G. (2011). Empathy and bullying: Exploring the influence of callous unemotional traits. Child Psychiatry & Human Development, 42(2), 183-196.

Patrick, D. L., Bell, J. F., Huang, J. Y., Lazarakis, N. C., & Edwards, T. C. (2013). Bullying and quality of life in youths perceived as gay, lesbian, or bisexual in Washington State, 2010. American Journal of Public Health, 103(7), 1255-1261

Peeters, M., Cillessen, A. H. N. & Scholte, R. H. J. (2010). Clueless or powerful? Identifying subtypes of bullies in adolescence. Journal of Youth and Adolescence, 39(10), 1041-1052.

Rigby, K. & Smith, P. K. (2011). Is school bullying really on the rise? Social Psychology of Education: An International Journal, 14(4), 441-455

Sinyor, M., Schaffer, a., & Cheung, A (2014). An observational study of bullying as a contributing factor in youth suicide in Toronto. Canadian Journal of Psychiatry, 59(12), 631-638.

Tippett, N. & Wolke, D. (2014). Socioeconomic status and bullying: A meta- analysis. American Journal of Public Health, 104(6), e48-e59

AN URGENT LOOK AT CYBERBULLYING

Cyberbullying is a more recent form of bullying and is probably a more insidious form than the original face-to-face bullying. Cyberbullying is any form of bulling activity that is carried out digitally. Cyberbullying therefore intrudes on individual privacy and exposes that person to the world through the various media.

With these technologies being so widespread today, there is even greater likelihood that any young person may be faced with cyberbullying at one time or another. According to a Pew Center Research study, "59% of U.S. teens have been bullied or harassed online, and a similar share says it's a major problem for people their age" (Anderson, September 27, 2018). With these statistics, young people must take some responsibility for ensuring that they do all in their power to prevent being a victim of cyberbullying and to prevent others from being bullied online. This current digital revolution and the resulting widespread cyberbullying make it all the more important why young people need to know how to prevent cyberbullying from happening, with the knowledge that 'prevention is better than cure'.

WHAT DOES CYBERBULLYING INVOLVE?

Cyberbullying takes place through social media, mobile phones as well as through message and gaming platforms (UNICEF, 2020).

This use of a variety of technologies makes it relatively easy for people to engage in cyberbullying. Reports also reveal that social media sites and apps are the most commonly used means of cyberbullying, and that they account for almost one-fifth of all cyberbullying (Cook, July 3, 2020). Other means include text messaging, internet other than social networking sites, cell phones and emails.

Basically, cyberbullying involves sending hurtful messages and threats through message platforms, posting embarrassing pictures about a person on social media, and using another person's identity to send mean messages to others (UNICEF, 2020). The most common forms of cyberbullying that were identified by teens in the Pew Center Research study were name-calling (42%), spreading of false rumors (32%), sharing of explicit images (25%), constant inquiry by someone other than a parent as to where they were and what they were doing (21%), and physical threats (16%) (Anderson, September 27, 2018). These were found to be carried out mostly through "texting and digital messaging" (Anderson, September 27, 2018).

Also, cyberbullying victims may receive harassing phone calls or may be harassed while on a chat line or forum. They may also receive threats and their friends and acquaintances may also be threatened or sent false information about them.

It is also possible that victims of cyberbullying could be excluded from social networking groups. All of these are deliberate actions to cause hurt to those that are targeted as victims of cyberbullying.

WHO ARE THE CYBERBULLIES?

Cyberbullies are often individuals who know their victims in some way but who may not be recognized as such by their victims. Cyberbullies may even be offline bullies, just looking for more ways to harass their offline victims. As one cyber security expert explains, there are really two types of cyberbullies: school bullies and cybercriminals out to make a profit (Cucu, April 24, 2017). As mentioned above, cyberbullies could target their victims in a chatroom or may incite others to bash their victims as well. Cyberbullies may use messaging such as Messenger and WhatsApp to abuse their victims repeatedly. Cybercriminals, on the other hand, may be more interested in getting nude pictures and using these to demand ransoms or favours (Cucu, April 24, 2017).

SOME TACTICS CYBERBULLIES USE

It is important to understand the tactics that cyberbullies use in order to oppose them. Cybercriminals often take on fake personas in order to attract their victims. For example, if the target victim is female, the cybercriminal may pose with a male persona and try to seduce the female victim. A similar strategy may be used for a male victim, with a female persona used to seduce the male.

Young people have to be aware of these tactics and realize that cyberbullying can start off as flattery to gain their trust, before it becomes abuse. Therefore, teenagers and young adults must take responsibility for not being seduced online. They should be aware that the identity and possible appearance of the person they have in mind when initially interacting with a cyberbully may be very different from the identity and appearance of the real person online.

URGENCY IN DEALING WITH CYBERBULLYING

Why is there such urgency surrounding cyberbullying? One of the major reasons is that this is a global issue and one that continues to increase. From self-reported studies on cyberbullying in the United States received over the period from 2007 to 2019, Cyberbullying Research Center reveals an average of 28% of teens reporting having been cyberbullied (Patchin, July 10, 2019).

In an Ipsos international study, where adults from 28 countries were surveyed, parents reported that their children were being bullied, with the top three countries being India (37%), Brazil (29%) and the United States (26%), and the three lowest countries being Russia (1%), Japan (5%), and Chile (8%) (Cook, July 3, 2020). Of Canada's parents surveyed, 20% reported having a child being cyberbullied. The rates of parents reporting cyberbullying of their children were 18% in Great Britain; 17% in China; 14% in Germany; 12% in Italy; 9% in Spain; and 9% in France; other countries showed varying percentages (Cook, July 3, 2020). This shows the global nature of this problem.

But there is an even more serious problem associated with cyberbullying. Reporting on a study carried out by Javelin Research, Cook (July 3, 2020) points to the finding that "children who are bullied are 9 times more likely to be victims of identity fraud as well" (Cook, July 3, 2020). What this suggests is that cyberbullying is a major problem that needs to be seriously addressed.

While young people must try to take all the precautionary measures to protect themselves, this is a societal problem that needs to be addressed by governments, owners of social media sites, app developers, and the owners and operators of other program delivery sites. Many young people believe that they are not getting sufficient support to fight this problem of cyberbullying. In the same Pew Center Research study mentioned earlier, the young people that were surveyed "mostly think teachers, social media companies and politicians are failing at addressing this issue" (Anderson, September 27, 2018).

One of the immediate problems is that "[m]ost victims do not share their bullying experience, and if they did, only half believe they are taken seriously. Both bullying among students in school and cyberbullying deserve attention due to their potentially devastating effects on victims" (Gan, Zhong, Das, Gan, Willis, & Tully, 2014).

ALL PARTIES NEED TO HAVE A HAND IN STOPPING CYBERBULLYING

This wide availability to various digital technologies means that a person can be bullied anywhere, even at home, at school, or in any venue, and when using any of these platforms. The very nature of cyberbullying makes it a practice that needs to be addressed urgently. As one source points out, cyberbullying is 'persistent', 'hard to detect', 'anonymous', and capable of spreading to a wide audience over a short period of time (Pacer's National Bullying Prevention Center (n.d.). This also means that cyberbullying could continue for a long time, as some of the materials created could remain on the Internet almost indefinitely.

IMPACT ON CYBERBULLYING VICTIMS - REPUTATION

One of the major impacts of cyberbullying is the fact that it can destroy the reputation of its victims. Since cyberbullying often leaves permanent materials behind, it causes harm for a long time. For some, this could be a lifetime impact not only on employment and other work situations, but also on friendships and other social relationships. The permanence of cyberbullying means that "it can be challenging to completely delete information once it is on the internet", but its permanence can be useful in that the incidents of cyberbullying can be documented (Pacer's National Bullying Prevention Center, 2020). This documentation of cyberbullying can be used to try to trace the origin of the cyberbullying and possibly deal with it. Except cyberbullying is stopped, it will continue to wreak havoc on many innocent lives, often with detrimental consequences.

OTHER IMPACTS ON INDIVIDUALS

There are several other impacts on young people who are victims of cyberbullying.

ANGER, SHAME, HUMILIATION AND LOSS OF TRUST

Cyberbullying inspires various feelings in victims. It gives the person being bullied the feeling of having no safe haven to which to retreat. With this loss of privacy, a victim of cyberbullying feels totally helpless, thoroughly victimized, and exposed to the world. Besides, this person feels anger, shame, embarrassment, or humiliation, or all of these feelings. The victim is hurt significantly by the activities associated with cyberbullying.

The fact that the victim doesn't know who the bully is makes the cyberbullying activities even more distressing. There is an associated lack of trust.

MENTAL, EMOTIONAL, AND PHYSICAL IMPACTS

As one source points out, the impact of cyberbullying on victims could be mental, emotional and physical (UNICEF, 2020). Victims of cyberbullying experience mental anguish at having their reputation tarnished online for everyone to see. They also experience emotional distress because of a feeling of shame and they may also lose interest in many of the activities that they previously enjoyed. One author sees cyberbullying as contributing to emotional trauma (Reyneke, 2019). A research study showed that children and young adolescents developed negative self-cognitions and depression as a result of being victims of cyberbullying

(Cole, Zelbowitz, Nick, Martin, Roeder, Sinclair-McBride & Spinelli, 2016). The physical impacts of being victims of cyberbullying include loss of sleep and loss of appetite, both detrimental to health and mental functioning.

FRUSTRATION AND HELPLESSNESS

There are also feelings of frustration. When victims of cyberbullying try to find out the identity of the bully, they often meet with roadblocks: technological and otherwise. Overall, victims of cyberbullying often experience feelings of helplessness that could challenge their mental health.

SOCIAL ISOLATION

Victims of cyberbullying who previously were very active on social media sites no longer go on these sites for fear of being laughed at or even ridiculed.

REASONS FOR CYBERBULLYING

There are several reasons why some people engage in cyberbullying. It could be that they are angry at the person for something or they may be angry at someone else, but decide to take it out on a more vulnerable person. There is also the possible case of revenge, where one person decides to cyberbully another person because of something that person may have done or said. Cyberbullies may simply want to show that they have power and are popular and use cyberbullying as evidence of their popularity. There is also the possibility that instead of confronting someone over an issue, one person may decide that it is better to avoid the confrontation but hurt the other person online. The decision to cyberbully could also stem from jealousy, where one person decides to spread false rumors about another person of whom he or she is jealous. There is no justifiable reason for engaging in cyberbullying against anyone.

MEASURES IN PLACE TO DEAL WITH CYBERBULLYING

As mentioned earlier, some young people believe that their teachers, governments and social media sites can be doing more to stop cyberbullies. One important consideration is to examine what these individuals and authorities are really doing to deal with cyberbullying.

MEASURES IN PLACE TO DEAL WITH CYBERBULLYING: GOVERNMENTS AND LEGAL CONSIDERATIONS

What measures are governments taking to deal with cyberbullying? One point of interest is that cyberbullying is considered a crime in many countries, including the United States and Canada. This is attested to by the fact that in the United States 49 of the states have passed cyberbullying laws, intended to punish bullies and to discourage this practice (Green, March 26, 2020). These laws for the most part require schools boards to take action by incorporating cyberbullying into their existing bullying policies (Green, March 26, 2020). Some states have also created misdemeanor offences for some cyberbullying activities. It seems that the school boards are given the responsibility for dealing with cyberbullying as well as with bullying in schools. But the misdemeanor offences may not be very effective in prosecuting cyberbullies.

In Canada, there are several laws that govern cyberbullying. In cyberbullying where people's physical images are shown online without their consent, this is considered an offence under Canada's Criminal Code (Public Safety Canada, 2018). Other laws that could be used to deal with cyberbullying under the Criminal Code include those covering offenses dealing with criminal harassment, uttering threats, intimidation, mischief in relation to data, defamatory libel, false messages, indecent or harassing phone calls, identity fraud, extortion, incitement of hatred, counselling suicide, and unauthorized use of a computer (Public Safety Canada, 2018).

Individual provinces also have cyberbullying prevention acts. For example, the province of Manitoba passed the Cyber-bullying Prevention Act, which empowers the victim to apply for protection order (Goertzen, 2013). With proper sworn evidence, the court has the power through the cyberbullying prevention act to prevent the bully from accessing electronics (Goertzen, 2013).

ARE GOVERNMENT MEASURES EFFECTIVE ENOUGH

Although in the United States there are cyberbullying acts, it appears that these laws deal more with delegating responsibility to school boards to establish effective anti-bullying policies. In Canada, although many of the cyberbullying activities are covered under Criminal Code legislation, this does not seem effective enough to prevent cyberbullying from taking place. As a Working Group of the government looking into cyberbullying legislation in Canada points out, many of the criminal code provisions are not modernized enough to deal with the expanding new digital technologies and so need revamping (Government of Canada, Department of Justice, January 19, 2017). Besides, the Working Group recommended certain revamping and expansion of certain sections of the Criminal Code to make the laws more focused to prosecute cyberbullying activities. Similarly, some foreign countries do not have strong modernized stand-along legislation that could fully prosecute cyberbullies.

MEASURES IN PLACE TO DEAL WITH CYBERBULLYING:

SOCIAL MEDIA

In one of its campaigns against cyberbullying, UNICEF "brought together UNICEF specialists, international cyberbullying and child protection experts, and teamed up with Facebook, Instagram and Twitter to answer the questions and give their advice on ways to deal with online bullying" (UNICEF, n.d.). These are some of the responses by Facebook, Instagram and Twitter about their efforts to deal with cyberbullying.

Facebook's response to cyberbullying is that anyone who is being bullied on the social media platform should "send our team an anonymous report from a post, comment or story on Facebook or Instagram" (UNICEF, n.d.). Facebook is also said to provide a guide on its site regarding how to deal with cyberbullying. A victim of cyberbullying can follow through with the process of reporting the incident through this guide. If cyberbullying takes place on Instagram, the victim or victim's parents could consult the Parent's Guide on the site which also provides information on how to follow through with reporting cyberbullying (UNICEF, n.d.). For Twitter, reports on cyberbullying could be made through the Help Center or by clicking on "Report a Tweet" on Twitter's in-tweet reporting system (UNICEF, n.d.). Friends can also help in reporting incidents on these social networking sites.

It was also reported that Facebook and Instagram also use AI technology which users can turn on. People could use the tool, "Restrict" which is "a tool designed to empower you to discreetly protect your account while still keeping an eye on a bully" (UNICEF, n.d.).

But while some of these measures may help, some young people may not know where to find these tools and may be unfamiliar with them. In some instances, getting through the measures to reporting on social media could be quite tedious and challenging.

MEASURES YOUNG PEOPLE CAN TAKE TO DEAL WITH CYBERBULLYING

Some measures victims of cyberbullying can take to deal with the situation are to tell someone about a cyberbullying incident; make a screenshot and save the evidence of the cyberbullying; don't engage with the cyberbully online; try to identify the bully; if in immediate danger, contact law enforcement; and always protect your information.

TELL SOMEONE

The rationale behind telling someone is that generally young people may not want to speak to their parents about their cyberbullying, but they may tell a friend or another adult.

TAKE SCREENSHOTS AND SAVE EVIDENCE

Young people are also encouraged to take screenshots of inappropriate behavior, in emails, text messages, posts, web pages, or photos and sometimes to even print things out.

In doing these things, young people who are victims of cyberbullying would have evidence that something happened. It is important to secure the date of the cyberbullying, as well as information about the sender and other vital details (Pacer's National Bullying Prevention Center, 2020).

DON'T ENGAGE WITH THE CYBERBULLY

Cyberbully victims are encouraged not to respond to anything that the bully may have included during the cyberbullying incident. The rationale is that the young person would not fall further prey to cyberbully.

TRY TO IDENTIFY THE CYBERBULLY

Besides telling someone and saving the information about the cyberbullying incident, a cyberbullying victim must try to identify the bully. Why is this important? As noted, "[f]or bullying to stop, it needs to be identified and reporting it is key. It can also help to show the bully that their behaviour is unacceptable" (UNICEF, n.d.).

CONTACT LAW ENFORCEMENT, IF IN IMMEDIATE DANGER

If the victims of cyberbullying feel they are in immediate danger, the next step to address cyberbullying is to contact police or emergency services in one's jurisdiction. In this case, it would be important to have as much information about the cyberbullying incident to provide to the police or other law enforcement agency.

PROTECT YOUR INFORMATION

Young people ought to be very careful about protecting their information online. They are advised to be careful about what they share as this may stay online forever. In this case, information provided in the past could come back to haunt the person posting that information. Further, young people are told not to put personal information as address, phone number and name of school on their sites.

They are also told to adjust the privacy levels on their profiles and limit those who can see, send direct messages and comment on posts. Young people with social networking sites can also delete posts from their profiles.

BUT LAWS MAY NOT BE ENOUGH

But even with these laws in place and with social networking sites claiming to provide anti-cyberbullying measures, cyberbullying still occurs. As noted: "It is important to note that no legislation will eliminate cyber-bullying and no legislation replaces the importance of parental involvement in the lives of youth that fosters respect and compassion for all people" (Goertzen, 2013). Another source also questions the utility of the law in curbing bullying. It is being argued that while the punishment for some offenses is jail, many young people do not report the matter and so cyberbullying is still alive and well. As Butler (2010) notes, sending someone to jail does not solve the problem. What this author recommends is more of a public education campaign and a "national conversation about the importance of civility and respect" rather than prison for manslaughter in the case where cyberbullying led to the death of the victim (Butler, 2010).

CONCLUSION

Friends and parents of individuals who are contemplating cyberbullying should take action. Young people who become aware that their friends may be planning to engage in cyberbullying for whatever reason should discourage them from doing so. Parents who are aware or who learn that their children are cyberbullies should take measures to stop this activity.

Individuals who have engaged in cyberbullying or who consider themselves cyberbullies should seek out professional help for their behaviour. Various therapists provide help for those who are victims of cyberbullying and for those who have done the cyberbullying. Seek these out immediately if you feel in crisis. Don't take your mental health for granted. Always seek out help when this is needed.

CHAPTER 5 - FOOD FOR THOUGHT

TOPICS AND IDEAS FOR SELF-REFLECTION AND
DISCUSSION

Self-Reflection

What would be the best strategy for me to use, if someone was being threatened with cyberbullying?

What would I do if I knew someone was being cyberbullied but tried to keep it a secret?

Group Discussion

Design an anti- cyberbullying prevention program that a group or class could institute in the community or school?

How would you implement it in a small community and in a large city?

Discuss the various types, consequences, and supportive measures that could be given to a young person who became a victim of a cyberbullying campaign.

CHAPTER 5 - REFERENCES AND FURTHER READING

11 Facts about Cyberbullying (n.d.) Do Something Organization. Available at https://www.dosomething.org/us/facts/11-facts-about-cyber-bullying

Anderson, M. (September 27, 2018). A majority of teens have experienced some form of cyberbullying. Pew Center Research. Available at https://www.pewresearch.org/internet/2018/09/27/a-majority-of-teens-have-experienced-some-form-of-cyberbullying/

Butler, P. (December 3, 2010). New criminal laws aren't the answer to bullying. New York Times. Available at https://www.nytimes.com/roomfordebate/2010/09/30/cyberbullying-and-a-students-suicide/new-criminal-laws-arent-the-answer-to-bullying

Cole, D. A., Zelkowitz, R. L., Nick, E., Martin, N. C., Roeder, K. M., Sinclair- McBride, K. & Spinelli, T. (2016). Longitudinal and incremental relation of cybervictimization to negative self-cognitions and depressive symptoms in young adolescents. Journal of Abnormal Child Psychology, 44(7), 1321-1332.

Cook, S. (July 3, 2020). Cyberbullying facts and statistics for 2020. Comparitech. Available at https://www.comparitech.com/internet-providers/cyberbullying-statistics/

Cucu, P. (April 24, 2017). Cyberbullying: facts, statistics and how to stop and prevent it: Keep your teenager safe on the Internet as well. Heindal Security. Available at https://heimdalsecurity.com/blog/how-to-stop-and-prevent-cyberbullying/

Gan, S. S., Zhong, C., Das, S., Gan, J. S., Willis, S., & Tully, E. (2014). The prevalence of bullying and cyberbullying in high school: a 2011 survey. International Journal of Adolescent Medicine and Health, 26(1), 27-31.

Goertzen, K. (July 18, 2013). Real measures to deal with cyberbullying. Available at https://www.mysteinbach.ca/blogs/4513/real-measures-to-deal-with-cyber-bullying/

Government of Canada, Department of Justice (January 19, 2017). Cyberbullying and the non-consensual distribution of intimate images. Available at https://www.justice.gc.ca/eng/rp-pr/other-autre/cndii-cdncii/p5.html

Hinduja, S. (September 1, 2020). Tik Tok: Pros, cons, and the promise of youth empowerment. Cyberbullying Research Center. Available at https://cyberbullying.org/tiktok-pros-cons-youth-empowerment

Macariola, J. (August 13, 2020). Cyberbullying – what it is, why it happens, and what parents can do. Techaddiction. Available at http://www.techaddiction.ca/cyber-bullying-signs.html

Pacer's National Bullying Prevention Center (n.d.) Cyberbullying: What parents should know. Available at https://www.pacer.org/bullying/resources/publications/protecting-child-from-cyberbullying.asp

Patchin, J. W. (July 10, 2019). Summary of our cyberbullying research (2007-2019). Cyberbullying Research Center. Available at https://cyberbullying.org/summary-of-our-cyberbullying-research

Reyneke, R. P. (2019). A Restorative approach to address cyber bullying. In Kowalczuk-Waledziak, M., Korzeniecka-Bondar, A., Danilewicz, W. & Lauwers, G. (2019). Rethinking teacher education for the 21st century. Verlag Barbara Budrich.

Public Safety Canada (October 4, 2018_. What is cyberbullying? Available at https://www.publicsafety.gc.ca/cnt/ntnl-scrt/cbr-scrt/cbrbllng/prnts/cbrbllng-en.aspx

Royal Canadian Mounted Police (February 21, 2019). Bullying and cyberbullying: learning resources. Available at https://www.rcmp-grc.gc.ca/cycp-cpcj/bull-inti/bullres-resinti-eng.htm

Shockness, I. (2020). Respect is Only Human: A Response to Disrespect and Implicit Bias. Toronto: Vanquest Publishing. Vol. 6. https://SuccessfulYouthLiving.com.

UNICEF (n.d.). Cyberbullying: what is it and how to stop it? Available at https://www.unicef.org/end-violence/how-to-stop-cyberbullying

UN News (September 4, 2019). A third of young people polled by UN report being a victim of online bullying. United Nations. Available at https://news.un.org/en/story/2019/09/1045532

U.S. Government (n.d.). Prevent Cyberbullying: Stop bullying. Be Aware of what your kids are doing. Available at https://www.stopbullying.gov/cyberbullying/prevention

TAKING RESPONSIBILITY BEHIND THE WHEEL

So you have reached the age where you can drive? Good for you! Reaching the legal age to drive does not necessarily mean having the maturity to be a responsible driver. Are you ready for the responsibilities that go with driving? Driving does not entail just getting into the car and zooming down the road, going at the maximum speed possible! Reaching the legal driving age and getting a license to drive also entail taking responsibility for following regulations and obeying traffic rules. It doesn't matter that there are no traffic enforcement officials around all the time. In fact, becoming a licensed driver demands that you become a defensive driver as well.

DON'T RUSH IT

Don't rush it. Your friends may be all rushing out to get their licenses. If you do not feel like doing it, if you do not feel ready, don't be pressured into getting a license. Don't feel that because your 18-year old friend, Stu, has a car and a license that you must have a car and license. Driving is a serious matter, which requires maturity, consideration, and clear thinking. Only when you feel you have these characteristics should you consider going for your license.

You may already have gotten your license, and you are really excited about it. You think it is really an accomplishment!

Now you can drive, and you can go wherever you want, whenever you want, if you have access to a car. Or maybe you already have your own car.

LOOK OUT FOR TEMPTATIONS

There would be temptations along the way. You may feel like showing off to your friends, especially to those who haven't gotten their licenses yet, or to those who do not have access to a car. You may want to compete with your friends who also have their licenses and their own cars.

AVOID IMMATURE AND DANGEROUS BEHAVIOR

You may be tempted, once behind the wheel, to speed, to show that you are really a competent driver, not like the 'scary cats' who are afraid to drive fast! This is foolish! You may be tempted to show 'older' drivers that your reflexes are better than theirs, that you can think faster than they can, and that you are a better driver than they are! You may be tempted to cut in and out of traffic to show that you can think and act fast! You may be tempted to change lanes right in front of another car, knowing that you can do it! You may be tempted to be the first one out as soon as the light changes to green, without delaying a minute or two as many 'slow' drivers do! Or you may be tempted to show that you can be the last one through when the light turns red! You may be tempted to challenge other drivers to dare to go faster than you can, knowing that you are prepared to go as fast as you have to in order to prove your point. All of this is immature and dangerous behavior.

FEEL INVINCIBLE ON THE ROAD?

Or you may feel like calling other drivers names if they do not get out of your way, or you may even feel like fighting with them, if they try to caution you about what they see as your irresponsible driving habits! You may think "road rage" is a sign of being an adult. You are wrong! It makes you look silly and immature! If you think this kind of behavior makes others look up to you, you are dead wrong. It makes you look like an insecure bully, and if you don't change your ways, you may even end up being 'dead'!

DON'T BE TEMPTED

Don't be tempted! Any of these temptations could mean DEATH to you, and to other innocent and responsible drivers and pedestrians. Speeding, frequently and unsafely changing lanes, jumping green lights, running red lights, challenging drivers on the road, and displaying road rage, are all habits that could cause deadly accidents or unnecessary incidents on the road. Even when another driver may try to challenge you to a race, don't be tempted! It is not worth it. Almost daily there are reports of people doing stupid things on the road and paying with their lives, or causing death or injury to innocent, law-abiding people. For one minute of fun, or one minute of feeling that you are invincible, you can lose your life, or cause the loss of another person's life.

"I DO THIS ALL THE TIME AND NOTHING HAPPENS!"

Some people may argue, "I do this all the time and nothing happens!" Or you may think, "That can't happen to me!" If you have done any of these things in the past, look out. There is that one day coming when you may not be so lucky. Maybe one day when you go to change lanes, there may be someone else doing the same thing. There may be that one day when you think you have just enough time to show off your driving prowess by running the red lights that another car may appear from nowhere. You may be in a fatal collision. Or maybe there is a car that is caught in the intersection and needs that extra minute to get out of the way, but there you are, not only running the lights, but going so fast that you can't even stop! That could surely be catastrophic!

BUT THERE ARE CONSEQUENCES?

Think of the consequences. A one-minute mistake could change lives forever. There are thousands of grieving parents, children and other family members, boyfriends, and girlfriends, who are mourning the loss of loved ones, who did not have a second chance. Some of these were victims of other people's carelessness or irresponsibility. Some caused their own deaths by their irresponsible actions, thinking at the time that they were invincible. Statistics show that many of those who die in car accidents are young people, 16-, 17-, 18-, 19-year-olds, and even people in their early 20s, people who thought they were too young to die. Young males feature very heavily in this category, although young females make up these statistics, too.

DON'T BE A STATISTIC!

Don't be a statistic! Don't try to show off! Doing stupid things would only make you look stupid, not smart. However, today, more and more young people are showing that they are responsible, careful, and thoughtful. When you try to show off, you only show these young responsible drivers how very immature you really are! Rather than gaining their attention, interest, or respect, you lose out on all counts! You don't have to show off on the road to make people think well of you. They won't! They only see you as insecure with low self-esteem.

YOU ARE SMARTER THAN THAT

You are smarter than that! You are sure of yourself! You have confidence in who you are! You don't have to prove that you are important or worthy of attention and respect by showing off on the road. You are smart enough to know that the rules of the road are intended to keep everyone safe and alive, even you.

By following the rules, others will know what you are going to do. When you run lights, change lanes illegally, do not give the right signal, or do many of the stupid things that cost lives, you are actually depending on chance. If you do not communicate to the other drivers on the road what you are going to do, how do you expect them to know? You are smarter than all this. If, in the past, you had not thought about what you were doing, now you have the 'goods'. When you show off on the road, you are acting immaturely.

YOU KNOW: ROAD SAFETY IS YOUR RESPONSIBILITY

Remember, driving is a privilege, not a right. It is a privilege you can lose. Privileges also have responsibilities. So does driving. As a driver, you have the responsibility to use the road safely and obey all the rules. You are responsible for operating your vehicle with care. You are responsible for not jeopardizing the lives of others who are also using the road. Of course, you also have a responsibility to yourself and your loved ones not to jeopardize your life! If you do not treat driving as a privilege, you could lose your license, or worse, lose your life. You could also deny others the privilege of living if you drive irresponsibly.

ASK YOURSELF: ARE YOU A RESPONSIBLE DRIVER?

Think about this! Think seriously about what you do when you are on the road. Are you a responsible driver, who sees his or her license not as a right, but as a privilege? Are you a driver who doesn't have to be first, or the fastest, on the road? Are you a driver that is considerate to others? Are you a driver who pays attention to the rules of the road, who remains calm while behind the wheel?

ASK YOURSELF: ARE YOU A DEFENSIVE DRIVER?

Are you a defensive driver who is aware of what other drivers around you are doing? Are you a driver who is ready at a moment's notice to take defensive action to avoid being in an accident? Are you a defensive driver who realizes that driving is a privilege, who knows that you have an important responsibility to help keep the roadway safe, and who is not tempted by other drivers who want to show off their prowess on the road to participate in road races and the like?

BE THE SMART PERSON YOU ARE INTENDED TO BE

If you answer "Yes" to these questions, then, you can consider yourself a responsible driver, who is less likely to cause an accident or be in one, which could end in DEATH: yours or somebody else's. Always remember, you are not too young to die, so don't drive as though you are!

CHAPTER 6 - FOOD FOR THOUGHT

TOPICS AND IDEAS FOR SELF-REFLECTION AND
DISCUSSION

Self-Reflection

Being very honest with myself, what type of a driver am I?

How do I compare with other young drivers my age?

Are the young drivers that I know good drivers?

Have I ever engaged in dangerous driving?

Do I drive defensively?

Group Discussion

What would you do if someone challenges you to race them on the street?

What kinds of penalties should be given to young drivers who break the law and drive dangerously?

What are some of the skills drivers should have in order to be considered defensive drivers?

CHAPTER 6 - REFERENCES AND FURTHER READING

Gray, K. E. (September 2016). The Keys to Defensive Driving. Available at https://kidshealth.org/en/teens/driving-safety.html

National Safety Council (2020). Teens' Biggest safety Threat is Sitting on the Driveway. Available at https://www.nsc.org/road-safety/safety-topics/teen-driving

"DRINKING AND DRIVING NOT A PROBLEM FOR ME: I CAN HOLD MY LIQUOR!"

DEADLY MYTHS EXPOSED

Despite the fact that the word is out, "Drinking and driving are a deadly combination," far too many people continue to combine the two. Many people claim that they can drink and drive because they have the ability to drink and not be impaired. They believe this myth, giving rise to too many drunk drivers on the road.

DRINKING AND DRIVING CAN BE DEADLY

However, while there are those who believe that drinking and driving could be deadly, they do not believe that their action could result in an accident, because they believe that even though they may drink, they are still in control of their abilities. Many people will tell you that they had only a small drink, or that they did not intend to drink and drive. They may explain that they went out with friends and may have had a little too much alcohol, but it was not serious! Others may say they know they can have a drink or two and still drive well. They believe it is other people who cannot 'hold their liquor' that should not drink and drive.

Then, there are others who are alcoholics, who know that they have a drinking problem and still drink and drive. This is not only selfish; it is irresponsible!! Don't rationalize your drinking. IF YOU DRINK, DON'T DRIVE. It is as simple as that. If you are under the legal age of drinking, don't drink. It doesn't make you more grown-up to consume alcohol.

DRINKING IMPAIRS JUDGEMENT AND GOOD SENSE

However, several studies have been carried out by academic researchers, health institutes, and organizations against drunk driving, which support the following claims: drinking impairs judgment; drinking impairs reflexes; and drinking impairs good sense. In short, drinking impairs the individual in all respects.

HAVING A GOOD TIME DOESN'T HAVE TO MEAN GETTING DRUNK

Unfortunately, in our society, drinking is usually associated with having a good time, which does not have to be the case. Many people, young and old, have a good time without drinking when they go out. However, a large part of our society subscribes to the use of alcoholic beverages as a condition for having fun, and many young people, eager to be considered grown-up, see this as a necessary condition for their social activities, even when they are not old enough to drink.

LOWER LEVEL OF IMPAIRMENT TOLERATED FOR YOUTH

Please note, if you are a young driver under the age of 21 (and if the law allows you to drink at all in your state), the law in most parts of the United States tolerates a very low level of impairment approximating zero, much lower than the 0.08% impairment in the blood alcohol concentration allowed for adults!!

Remember, if you are 21 and over, you are an adult, fully responsible for your actions, and fully responsible for the decisions you make. Make wise decisions, and remember that poor decisions have serious consequences for your life and the lives of other innocent people. So, please don't be selfish! Don't drink and drive!!

IF YOU DRINK, HAVE A DESIGNATED DRIVER

When you go out with friends, if you are old enough to use alcoholic beverages, you may decide to drink. If this is the case, be prepared to take responsibility for your drinking. If you normally drive, go with someone who will be the designated driver for that day or evening. That person, to be considered the designated driver, must agree not to drink at all, and must live up to his or her agreement.

STICK TO YOUR PLAN - DON'T DRINK

If you are driving and you decided beforehand that you would not drink, then stick to your previous plans. If you are going to drink, and you have a car, make sure that you make arrangements to leave your car at home and use a taxi or bus. If you have a responsible family member who would drop you off at the event, this may be a good decision.

LEAVE YOUR CAR WHERE IT IS PARKED

If you drive to the party and drink while you are there, you may be making the best decision to leave your car where you parked it at the party and take other transportation home. You can always retrieve your car later.

HAVING BREAKFAST THE MORNING AFTER MAY NOT BE ENOUGH

You may argue that if you drink and then stay at the party for a certain amount of time before you leave, then you would well be in control of all of your faculties to drive safely home. You may believe that your blood alcohol concentration (BAC) would be low enough that you would not be driving intoxicated. You may think that even if you were pulled over, you could not be found guilty of driving while intoxicated – driving under the influence (DUI). For those who may drink excessively, they may believe that if they stayed over after the party, slept, and ate breakfast the following morning, they would definitely be capable of driving home the following morning without breaking the law.

COMPUTING YOUR BAC IS NOT VERY ACCURATE

Computing your BAC is not a very accurate procedure, although it is based on how much time it takes for alcohol to be metabolized in the human body. Several formulas and procedures exist to guide an individual in calculating how much alcohol is still in the body after drinking. However, how your body functions will vary based on age, weight, gender, how long you had been drinking and how much you drank. It will also depend on your knowledge of how much alcohol you are consuming in the punches and alcoholic beverages you are consuming. Calculating also depends on your ability to do the math required to tell you how much time is needed for the alcohol you consumed to be metabolized, or even for your body to have the legally allowable limit. This would also depend on you having all the accurate information about the alcoholic content in your drinks.

BAC MAY DIFFER FOR SIMILAR BODIES

Even being able to calculate your BAC is no guarantee that you are accurate. The issue with not knowing how different bodies react to, and metabolize, alcohol also adds to the complications. This means that two people following the same schedule in drinking may have different BAC at the same time, because of differences in their bodies. This has serious implications, which means that you cannot be sure whether all the alcohol is out of your body, or at least when you have the lowest possible legal BAC reading which is 0.08, or closer to zero when you are not yet an adult.

Researchers have found that a majority of the serious motor vehicle crashes involving young people occur when they are within the legal BAC reading of 0.08. It was also noted that even after young people may have slept and had breakfast after a night of binge drinking, they were still impaired the following morning, and unfit to drive. All of this information is also relevant for older adults.

INCIDENCE OF DRINKING AND DRIVING STILL TOO HIGH

Recent research studies in both the United States and Canada have shown that while the practice of drinking and driving among young people in both countries has declined over the past ten years that the incidence of impaired driving among this group is still too high. While there is still too much drinking and driving taking place, there is a more serious problem with the use of drugs. The legalization of marijuana in some states and provinces, though hailed as long overdue by some observers, poses serious challenges when young people use drugs and drive.

CHARGED WITH DUI NOT SMART

With the costs so high for driving when impaired, being charged with a DUI, being found to be impaired with drugs, and causing a fatal accident in which innocent people are killed, or in which the drivers are often being killed, intelligent young people are called upon to do the sensible thing of simply making sure not to be impaired behind the wheel. Several scenarios were given earlier to avoid this.

RECKLESS AND SELFISH – FOUR PEOPLE DEAD

Today, as I write this, a 29 year-old man, who had received several tickets and warnings within the past few months in different jurisdictions for dangerous driving, speeding, and drinking and driving, crashed into a minivan carrying three children under ten years old, a grandfather, grandmother, and great-grandmother. The 29-year old killed the children and grandfather, and seriously injured the other two. While he escaped with only minor scratches, he is now facing 18 counts for his recklessness and selfishness, and would very likely spend several years behind bars. He was returning from his stag party and was to be married a week later. All of his life plans are ruined by drinking and driving, by speeding and driving dangerously. Was this really worth it?

A COMMON-SENSE TOPIC?

While this topic of drinking and driving may appear a commonsense topic that every young person has heard about and should understand, for some reason it is often ignored and pushed under the carpet, until something tragic happens.

YOU ARE INTELLIGENT AND RESPONSIBLE

As an intelligent and responsible young person, bring this up as a topic for discussion among your friends. After all, the price for driving under the influence (DUI) is just too great.

CHAPTER 7 - FOOD FOR THOUGHT

TOPICS AND IDEAS FOR SELF-REFLECTION AND DISCUSSION

Self-Reflection

What would I do if one of my friends is drunk and decides to drive home?

What would I do if I know my friend has had several drinks for the night, and he assures me that he is sober and can drive?

Group Discussion

If your group is planning an Old Year's Party and you are in charge of planning, what are some of the measures you would take in order to prevent members trying to drive home drunk?

CHAPTER 7 - REFERENCES AND FURTHER READING

Li, K., Simons-Morton, B.G., Hingson, R. (2013). Impaired-driving prevalence among US high school students: Associations with substance use and risky driving behaviors. *American Journal of Public Health, 103,* 71-77

O'Malley, P.M., Johnston, L.D. (2013). Driving after drug or alcohol use by US high school seniors, 2001 – 2011. *American Journal of Public Health, 103,* 2027-2034.

Pickett, W., Davison, C., Torunian, M., McFaull, S., Walsh, P. & Thompson, W. (2012). Drinking, substance use and the operation of motor vehicles by young adolescents in Canada. *PLOS ONE, 7*(8) 1-15.

Witty, H. (September 14, 2020). MADD turns 40: One Mom's impactful story. Available at https://goodlifefamilymag.com/2020/09/14/madd-turns-40-one-moms-impactful-story/

CHAPTER 8

HAVEN'T YOU HEARD? USING DRUGS AND DRIVING ALSO MAKES NO SENSE

WHY EXPERIMENT – YOU HAVE THE GOODS

Many young people experiment with alcohol and drugs. Although our society is more concerned about the use and abuse of illegal drugs, the truth is, alcohol is the drug that most children and young people experiment with first. This is so, because of the easy availability of alcohol in many homes. Young people could consume alcohol without their parents being aware of it.

TAKING DRUGS NOT A POPULARITY GAME

Some parents take alcohol use very lightly. Believing that they can make their older children more popular among other teenagers, some parents even provide alcohol for their older children's parties. Some teenagers confide that they are able to order alcohol from home. All of these factors contribute to young people and children having too easy access to alcohol.

FREE DRUGS AS INDUCEMENT

Illegal drugs are also readily available, if one knows the source. Those who deal in drugs endeavor to make their businesses more accessible to young people, and so recruit other young people to be sellers. In many instances, these drugs are provided free for students to try, the rationale being that once these students become addicted, they represent a captive market.

Even if young people do not work, they are often able to get the money for drugs. Some young people steal from family as well as from strangers to support their drug habit. Some bully other students and take away their money. Some young people from wealthy families can support their drug habit from their own resources. Unfortunately, these young people often do not experience the same scrutiny as their less affluent peers, and so can sometimes be at greater risk for drug addiction.

YOU ARE NOT IMMUNE TO ADDICTION

Even though many young people know that it is wrong for them to use alcohol or illegal drugs, many of them are curious. Even though they know drug use could lead to addiction, many young people often think that they can't become addicted. Some believe they can stop using whenever they want, only to be rudely awakened several weeks later to realize that they are seriously addicted to drugs. Many think of themselves as invincible, as beyond the reach of death, and continue in their addiction.

RESIST DRUG USE

Most schools have some kind of drug awareness program that would alert children and young people to the dangers of drug use. Despite these and other measures, drug use among young people is commonplace. Many high schools are taking measures to discourage such activity on their premises, by having under-cover police officers in the school, some of whom may serve in different capacities, the younger ones passing as students themselves. While students are aware that there may be a police officer in their midst, they could seldom identify him or her. It is the anonymity of the police officer that helps to keep some students in line, because they don't know when they may be caught.

DON'T BE FOOLED BY THE COMEBACK

However, even the threat of being caught does not faze some young people. They crave popularity and popularity often means running with the wild crowd, where illegal substances are often commonplace. Marijuana, which is the drug that has been used for centuries and which became less popular in light of newer drugs, is now making a comeback, especially with its legalization in some states and countries.

DON'T FOOL YOURSELF – MEDICAL MARIJUANA IS NOT FOR RECREATIONAL USE

Marijuana has been shown to have medicinal properties, as illustrated in the comprehensive study carried out by Dr. Sanjay Gupta on CNN (2015). The medical use of marijuana was shown to help control the serious illnesses of some children who could not be helped using conventional methods and treatments. In this and other reports on the medical use of marijuana, none of these professionals have advocated for the widespread use of marijuana for recreational use. Yet, many people, young and old alike, are now using medicinal values as justification for recreational use of this drug.

MARIJUANA USE JEOPARDIZES NORMAL BRAIN DEVELOPMENT

In the meantime, studies carried out on adolescent use of marijuana reveal that there is reason for young people to use caution, and if possible, avoid use of this drug. According to some researchers, young people who use marijuana and alcohol jeopardize normal development of the adolescent brain as there is potential for alteration in neurodevelopment (Jacobus, Squeglia, Ingante, Bava and Tapert, 2013). An earlier study also supports the claim that visuospatial working memory is compromised through the use of marijuana as young people demonstrate deficits in functioning in these areas (Smith, Longo. Fried, Hogan and Cameron, 2010). While the perceived risk of marijuana use is at an all-time low, people are starting to use marijuana at a younger age.

According to another study, "[a]s adolescence is a critical period of neuromaturation, teens and emerging adults are at greater risk for experiencing the negative effects of MJ (marijuana) on the brain" (Gruber, Dahlgren, Sagar, Gonenc and Lukas, 2014). One of the most notable of these negative impacts identified is being impulsive, which is associated with alteration of the white matter in the frontal part of the brain.

MARIJUANA EFFECT IN THE WOMB

A more recent study is even more damning, pointing out that when individuals are exposed to marijuana prenatally, these individuals are likely to become users of marijuana when they are quite young. Studies have found that individuals who were pre-exposed to marijuana before they were born were highly likely to develop psychotic symptoms in their adolescence (Day, Goldschmidt, Day, Larkby, and Richardson, 2015). In other words, young people who are engaged in early use of marijuana could also develop mental health issues as a result of their marijuana use and could be predisposed because of prenatal exposure to this drug. These are not findings to be ignored!!

A WORD ABOUT MARIJUANA USE AND DRIVING

Although marijuana does not present the same acute problem of impairment that alcohol does, there is still cause for concern with impairment related to use of marijuana and its impact on driving. With states like Colorado and Washington in the United States legalizing marijuana and several other states poised to follow suit, and with Canada considering passing similar legislation, there is concern that this could lead to a widespread problem of impaired driving related to marijuana use.

There have already been episodic reports of increased impaired driving in both the United States and Canada. Reports have shown that individuals driving under the influence of alcohol and marijuana are at greater risk of being involved in a collision than if the individual had used only one drug (Pacula, Kilmer, Wagenaar, Chaloupka and Caulkins, 2014). While there are some regulations in place as to how young people are judged to be impaired by drugs, this is not as clearly identified as in the case of alcohol. Yet, drug impairment is being prosecuted.

Just as in the case of alcohol impairment, so in the case of other drug impairment, young people need to take precaution because of the serious consequences on their future and their lives.

START A DISCUSSION

If you are a young person, start a discussion with your friends. The more young people see the connection between their actions and consequences, the safer our roads would be for all drivers and pedestrians, including you.

Discussion

Self-Reflection

How would I feel about using drugs and my parents and friends finding out?

How would I feel if any of my friends or family members died of an overdose?

How would I respond if my best friend told me he/she uses drugs?

What would I do?

Group Discussion

Read and discuss these quotes in class or in your group

"Drugs are a waste of time. They destroy your memory and your self-respect and everything that goes along with your self-esteem." - Curt Cobain.

Discuss what this means and discuss who Kurt Cobain was.

"Sobriety was the greatest gift I ever gave myself." – Rob Lowe

"My recovery is the single greatest accomplishment of my life. Without that, the rest of my life would have fallen apart." – Martin Sheen.

Why are these statements so important to young people?

CHAPTER 8 - REFERENCES AND FURTHER READING

Day, N.L., Goldschmidt, L., Day, R., Larkby, C. and
Richardson, G.A. (2015). Prenatal marijuana
exposure, age of marijuana initiation, and the
development of psychotic symptoms in young adults.
Psychological Medicine, 45, 1779-1787.

Gruber, S.A., Dahlgren, M.K., Sagar, K.A., Gonenc, A. and
Lukas, S.E. (2014). Worth the wait: effects of age of
onset of marijuana use on while matter and
impulsivity. *Psychopharmacology, 231,* 1455-1465.

Gupta, S. (2015). Dr. Sanjay Gupta: It's time for a medical
marijuana revolution.
*http://www.cnn.com/2015/04/16/opinions/medic
al-marijuana-revolution-sanjay-gupta/*

Jacobus, J., Squeglia, L.M., Infante, M.A., Bava, S. and
Tapert, S.F. (2013). White matter integrity pre- and
post-marijuana and alcohol initiation in
adolescence. *Brain Sciences, 3,* 396-414.

Melberg, H. O., Jones, A. M. & Bretteville-jensen, A. L.
(2010). *Empirical Economics, 38*(3), 583-603.

Pacula, R.L., Kilmer, B., Wagenaar, A.C., Chaloupka, F.J.,
and Caulkins, J.P. (2014). Developing Public Health
Regulations for Marijuana: Lessons from alcohol
and tobacco. *American Journal of Public Health,
104*(6). 1021-1032

Smith, A.M., Longo, C.A., Fried, P.A., Hogan, M.J. and
Cameron, I. (2010). Effects of marijuana on
visuospatial working memory: an MRI study in
young adults. *Psychopharmacology, 210,* 429-438.

CHAPTER 9

STEALING CARS AND JOYRIDING –

CRIMINAL AND COSTLY

Some youngsters see stealing cars and joyriding as teenage pranks to joke and boast about among their delinquent friends. Some young males see stealing cars and cruising with their girlfriends as accomplishments that demonstrate their manhood and ruggedness, and that make them more appealing to these girls. Still yet, other youngsters see this activity as a viable means of making money, by stripping stolen cars and selling the parts to shady characters with chop shops. Some young people even become involved inadvertently in organized crime, where theft of cars is seen as part of its operations.

NOT TEENAGE PRANKS OR SIGNS OF INGENUITY

Stealing cars and joyriding are not teenage pranks, neither are they indicative of manhood and ruggedness. Young women are sometimes implicated. Besides, these activities are far from being a viable way of making money or even a living. Rather, stealing cars and joyriding are criminal acts that could lead to death, causing untold heartaches for families and friends.

Stealing cars and joyriding also cause hardship and inconvenience, economic and otherwise, to those whose cars are stolen. These behaviors are usually the beginning of a career of increasing criminal activity with usually grave consequences for those who engage in the activities.

IT'S ONLY A MATTER OF TIME BEFORE ONE IS CAUGHT

Although many car thieves get away with stealing a car, sometimes once, twice, or even a few times, it is only a matter of time before the law catches up with them. Stealing cars and joyriding destroy a person's reputation. The person who steals a car may think he or she impresses others, but in most cases the person he or she really wants to impress may be disgusted with, or embarrassed by, his or her criminal acts. Friends who condone car theft and joyriding are not really friends. They are lost souls running towards their own destruction.

MY PERSONAL EXPERIENCE

Stealing cars and joyriding are criminal acts that could lead to death. A few days before Christmas a few years ago, I had just dropped off my two young children at school. It was their last school day before the Christmas holiday and it was to be a shortened day. I had promised to take them shopping later after lunch.

I started driving back home when I noticed a car that was behind me speed past me on the inside, and then pulled across the road in front of me a short distance ahead. I stopped abruptly, thinking, "What maniac is this on the road?" I was speechless, shaken up, and then dumbfounded, when I saw what could have happened. The car that had pulled across the road in front of me turned out to be an unmarked police car. The officer had intercepted a car that was coming directly towards me in my lane going the wrong direction. There was a collision between the police car and the oncoming car. All of this was unfolding in front of me.

As it turned out, it was a 14-year old girl who had staggered out of the car, stoned out of her mind with alcohol, drugs or both, and who had only shortly before stolen her mother's car and was taking it for a joy ride. Had the officer not been there, I could have been her first casualty. The officer, through his quick thinking, had averted a terrible accident, and saved my life that day, for which my family and I are forever grateful. On reflection, I was embarrassed for initially thinking of the officer in the unmarked car as a 'maniac'. In fact, he was an 'angel'.

STEALING CARS AND JOYRIDING ARE CRIMINAL ACTS

Stealing cars and joyriding are criminal acts that have great economic cost. One morning, I woke up to find my car was stolen out of my driveway. I reported the matter to the police. After waiting for several days, I got word that my car was recovered. My joy turned to horror when I saw that the car was stripped, smashed, dented and scratched in several places. The inside of the car was strewn with McDonald's cups, wrappers and other garbage, and a girl's pink stuffed-toy key-chain with its key still attached was on the back seat. I was thoroughly disgusted that my car was so destroyed and violated.

CAR THEFT COSTLY FOR CAR OWNER

This was a costly experience for me since I virtually lost my car, and with insurance only covering for a fraction of the cost of a new car, everyone lost. The thief probably got a few hours of joyriding for his or her effort, and I had to bear the additional cost of a car.

No One Is Impressed with a Car Thief!

Stealing cars and joyriding do not impress anyone, not even the ones riding with the thief. Whatever perverse pleasure these car thieves derive from their criminal acts lasts for a few hours, and then it's gone. So what has been gained? Besides, stealing cars actually destroys one's self-image.

It Makes No Sense

If you are a young person who got caught up in this type of activity, think about it. It makes no sense. Lives could be lost, yours included. People whose vehicles are stolen are forced to bear economic loss, and as the thief you get virtually nothing but a few hours of joyriding. Besides, you run the risk of a criminal record that could limit your life chances.

Change is Possible

However, you could change things. Tell yourself: "This is the end of the line for me. I'll change my ways!" Mean it. Judge Greg Mathis, a real judge as well as a TV judge, tells of his criminal past as a young person. However, he made a conscious decision one day to change his criminal ways, and it paid off. Today, he is on the other side of the law, trying to help young people to straighten out their lives. It's not too late for you.

TAKING RESPONSIBLE ACTION

Think about being responsible in your actions, and avoid getting involved in criminal activity, regardless of how attractive and fun-creating it may appear. Act as the smart person that you are meant to be. An hour of joyriding in a stolen car could mark the beginning of the end of your freedom. Even if you did it once and got away with it, think of the possible hardship that it caused others and the short-term fun that you may have experienced. Stealing cars and joyriding could change your life, which at the present time, may be full of promise, to a life of regret, imprisonment and failure. Recognize that decent young people stay in school and imitate good role models, as they try to be law-abiding. Well-informed and desirable young men and women recognize that being responsible involves not breaking the law, but acting in ways that promote a safe community.

YOU MAY BE A GOOD EXAMPLE

You may be a law-abiding young person who may never consider doing something as silly as this. However, through discussions with other young people, you may be able to reach out to others who may be misled into this behavior and may be able to convince them to change their ways.

CHAPTER 9 - FOOD FOR THOUGHT

TOPICS AND IDEAS FOR SELF-REFLECTION AND DISCUSSION

Self-Reflection

How would I feel if someone stole my car?

How would I feel if I found out that they took my car or my family car out for a joy ride?

If I were to meet that person, what would I say to him or her?

What action would I want to see taken against that person?

Group Discussion

Why do you think some young people steal cars and/or joyride?

How would you discourage a friend from getting involved in this activity? Or in getting out of such activity?

What group initiative can be used to discourage this activity among young people? What kind of content could be used in a brochure, for example, as a group campaign against car stealing by young people?

CHAPTER 9 - REFERENCES AND FURTHER READING

Mathis, G. (2002). *Inner City Miracle*. New York: Ballantine Books.

Wang, T. M., Loeber, R., Slotboom, A., Bijleveld, C. C., Hipwell, E. E. et al. (2013). Sex and age differences of the risk threshold for delinquency. *Journal of Abnormal Child Psychology, 41*(4), 641-652.

What stopped this kid from stealing cars? How one troubled teen turned his life around (October 11, 2017). New Zealand Herald. Available at https://www.nzherald.co.nz/nz/news/article.cfm?c_id=1&objectid=11931714

DATE RAPE IS A CRIME

Date rape is a common practice that is highly under-reported, according to police departments and women's groups. Shame, embarrassment, and fear of not being believed are some of the reasons young women do not report the incidents. Sometimes, when such reports have been made, a young man, accused, may mount a defense that the young woman did not protest, that she went along with it, or that he and the young woman previously had intimate relations. Consequently, date rape has prevented many young women who have been raped from speaking out.

SPEAKING UP

However, in recent months, probably because of greater willingness on the part of some young women to speak up, because of more opportunity for providing proof of communication, or because of social media that encourage some males to boast about their sexual exploits, there have been some high-profile cases of date rape on college and university campuses in the United States and Canada that have been brought to court and to public attention. For some of the males that have been accused and tried, the consequences have been severe, with some young males even serving jail time.

SOME CAUSES OF DATE RAPE

What causes date rape and rape in general? Several theories have been forwarded to explain this. One is the socialization theory, which holds that our culture supports men's use of force, and that men are socialized to get what they want by force. Another theory is the psychopathology theory, which holds that men who rape are maladjusted. Some feminist theories hold that rape is caused by the unequal power between men and women, with young men seeing their right to exercise control over young women and using young women for their pleasure.

All of these theories are relevant, since elements of these may be evident in the different cases of rape seen in society. But most important of all, young people, both men and women, are responsible for taking control of themselves. As an intelligent young person, you make decisions for yourself. Make the right choices.

CIRCUMSTANCES SURROUNDING DATE RAPE

What are the circumstances surrounding date rape? In some cases, young women have been raped using physical force. Other women have been drugged. In some of these date rape cases, women were found to be drugged and raped. Sexual assault squads from police departments and staff from women's clinics and health centers have noted an increase in the number of date rape cases in recent years. This increase in reports could result from a greater incidence of sexual abuse, or from a greater willingness on the part of young women to report these occurrences.

DATE RAPE DRUGS

Some of the drugs that are commonly used as date rape drugs are hallucinogens, some naturally occurring, but the majority are synthetic. The drugs that are commonly known as date rape drugs or club drugs include Rohypnol (flunitrazepam) and gamma hydroxybutyrate (GHB), as well as ketamine, MDMA (Ecstasy), methamphetamine and methaqualone or quaaludes. Other new synthetic drugs used in date rape are constantly entering the market. It is important to make sure not to use any of these drugs, or to give any of these drugs to others. While most of the cases of date rape involved women as victims, some young men are also reporting date rape by other men.

VICTIMS' REPORTS

Besides, the accounts given by date rape victims who had been drugged revealed that most of these victims experienced amnesia, but with the gnawing feeling afterwards that something terrible had happened to them. Some victims had only brief recollections of some of the incidents. In general, according to reports, it was difficult to detect, and in some cases, it was only a visit to a health center, a hospital or a doctor's office that indicated to these women that they had been drugged and raped. These reports come from victims and health centers in various parts of Canada and the United States.

YOUNG WOMEN, GUARD YOUR DRINKS

The practice of drugging women usually involves drinks, and this often takes place at a party, in a bar, or in another setting where alcoholic beverages are being served. When a young woman is not looking, her drink could be spiked with drugs. One recommendation to young women is that if they go to a party or other event, they should get their own drinks, be watchful as they finish these drinks, and never leave their drinks unattended or even with a friend to go to the bathroom or to dance.

NOT A CONQUEST, BUT A COWARDLY ACT

There is a message here for young men, too. If you have engaged in this practice in the past, be warned that date rape is not funny. It is nothing to be proud of, neither is it something to boast about to friends. It is not a conquest, but a cowardly act. It doesn't distinguish you as a man, but as a male who fails to control himself. Experts also tell us that rape is not a crime of sex, but a crime of violence, suggesting that rapists engage in violence.

PRESSURE AND INTIMIDATION ARE ALSO INVOLVED IN RAPE

When drugs are not used in a date rape, there are several different scenarios. In some instances, women are pressured, intimidated, or forced to engage in sexual activity. The usual perpetrator may be a classmate, work colleague, a special friend, or lover. In the case of adults, it could also be a spouse.

'NO' MEANS 'NO'

Other scenarios reveal that in some cases, there is miscommunication. In some instances, there is misinterpretation based on a sexist understanding of women. Some men believe that when a woman says "No," she is pretending to be modest, or she is teasing, and in reality, she really means "Yes." This is a myth that should be dispelled. When someone says "No," whether male or female, that person means "No."

PERSISTENCE DOES NOT PAY OFF IN CASE OF RAPE

Another scenario is where a woman enjoys the flattery of being pursued, but really does not want to be involved sexually. The young man, on the other hand, may misunderstand her actions as a sexual invitation.

There are instances where a young man knows that the young woman has objected to being involved in sexual activity, but persists, believing that he could use the excuse of miscommunication to get out of trouble, if it comes to that. In some recent court cases, this excuse has not worked.

YOUNG WOMEN, BE DIRECT, COMMUNICATE UNEQUIVOCALLY

Experts recommend that in these scenarios, a young woman should be very direct and communicate unequivocally that she is not interested in sexual involvement, and that to demonstrate this, she should remove herself from any situation that would suggest her willingness to engage in such activity. This means not only saying "No." It also means leaving a setting and giving an unequivocal message that she is not interested. If, as a young woman, you find yourself in this situation, make sure you do not give mixed signals.

RAPE CAUSES HARM IN SEVERAL WAYS

It is important to understand that rape or sexual assault causes harm in several ways. Rape causes physical and emotional harm to the young woman, with emotional harm often lasting a very long time. Some women never get over it. This experience often has a serious impact on all aspects of the young woman's life, for it could affect her studies, her subsequent relationships with other men, and much more. If young men are victims of rape, the impact could also be traumatic and have long-lasting consequences as well. There are consequences for young men, as the aggressors. If the young men as accused are convicted, this could mean jail time for them. All in all, date rape is a sinister practice that brings no one any good. Pay Attention.

Therefore, young women, always be aware of your surroundings, and if you drink, pay attention to your drinks. Also, use moderation and don't get drunk or impaired through drug use. You should also make sure that you are very clear when you say "No." Young men, be more respectful to young women and remember that "No" means "No." Date rape is a dangerous practice, for rape is a devastating experience that could affect a young person for life. It is also dangerous because if convicted, a young man could ruin his many life chances.

USE OF HARD DRUGS OFTEN ASSOCIATED WITH DATE RAPE

If you are a young person who is experimenting with these illegal drugs, think of the great risks you are taking. Firstly, you are subjecting your body to serious chemical substances. You are risking permanent damage and death in many instances. In recent weeks, there have been a rash of deaths through overdose. Secondly, since this is the only body you will have for the rest of your life, many of these chemical substances could remain in your body, and hurt your children, when you decide to become parents. Thirdly, you are taking the chance of being caught, of being thrown out of school, or of getting into trouble with the law. But use of illegal drugs has also been associated with date rape. Young men and women who use drugs often end up making impaired decisions. It is in circumstances like these that date rape often takes place.

IS IT WORTH IT?

These and other drugs do nothing for you, except harm you. Don't be a follower, and do what others want you to do. Be your own person. Be a leader, who is not afraid to be different from his or her peers, and who could influence his or her peers to do the right thing. Young men, recognize that date rape is a crime and do not follow along with others. Young women, know you have a responsibility to take charge of your body at all times. When you take drugs, you leave control to whoever wants to assume that control. Whether male or female, be responsible and have a conversation with your friends about this subject.

CHAPTER 10 - FOOD FOR THOUGHT

TOPICS AND IDEAS FOR SELF-REFLECTION AND DISCUSSION

Self-Reflection

DATE RAPE – "NO" MEANS "NO"

How would I feel if I were in this situation?

Either as the person who is thinking of not taking "No" for an answer? (which will involve an assault and is illegal)

Or as the person who says "No" and is the target of an assault?

What will happen if the act goes through?

What measures would I take to prevent myself from getting into this situation?

Group Discussion

How would you plan a class presentation on the subject?

What information would you gather for your presentation and how would you introduce the subject?

What advice would you give to someone who has had this experience?

CHAPTER 10 REFERENCES AND FURTHER READING

Black, K. A. & Gold, D. (2008). Gender differences and socioeconomic status biases in judgments about blame in date-rape scenarios. *Violence & Victims,* *23*(1), 115-128

Dodich, C. and Siedlarz, M. (2014). Date rape drugs. *International Journal of Child and Adolescent Health, 7* (4), 355-368

Foubert, J.D. & Newberry, J. T. (2006). Effects of two versions of empathy-based prevention program on fraternity men's survival empathy, attitudes and behavioral intent to commit rape or sexual assault. *Journal of College Student Development, 47*(2), 33-148

Hansen, S., O'byme, R. & Rapley, M. (2010). Young heterosexual men's use of the miscommunication model in explaining acquaintance rape. *Sexuality Research & Social Policy, 7*(1), 45-49

Hildenbrand-Gunn, T. L., Heppner, M. J., Mauch, P. A. & Park, H. (2010). Men as allies: the efficacy of a high school rape prevention intervention. *Journal of Counselling and Development, 88*(1), 43-53

Strain, M. L., Hockett, J. M., & Saucier, D. A. (2015). Precursors to rape: Pressuring behaviors and rape proclivity. *Violence & Victims, 30*(2), 322-341.

Shockness, I. (July 25, 2019). What part of "No" don't you understand? Successful Youth Living Blog. Available at https://www.successfulyouthlivingblog.com/2019/07/23/what-part-of-no-dont-you-understand

VOLUNTEERING AND YOUNG PEOPLE

Have you considered volunteering or do you volunteer at the present time? Some people believe that young people are more concerned with getting paid for their work and see volunteering as something best reserved for old retired individuals. This is not to say that young people are not volunteering at a number of organizations and supporting worthwhile causes. Statistics show that both in the United States and Canada, volunteering is on the increase among young people.

YOUTH VOLUNTEERING IN THE UNITED STATES

In the United States, more than half the young people, both teenagers and young adults, volunteer. Those between 13 and 22 were found to most often volunteer because their friends were volunteering, showing that they were very interested in spending time with friends and having the opportunity to meet other young people, particularly individuals of the opposite sex (Hall, 2012). A survey further reveals that twice as many young people volunteered for friendship as volunteered for a cause in which they believe.

The most common activity that these young people were shown to engage in was primarily fundraising. However, boys were also found to take part in manual activities, such as cleaning up the environment and working with younger children in sports.

Girls were more likely to work with the homeless, needy people, and art groups. Research also showed that young adults, for example, college and university students, were increasingly volunteering as they felt it was important to help people in need.

YOUTH VOLUNTEERING IN CANADA

In Canada, about 58% of young people between the ages of 15 and 24 were more likely to volunteer, with 15 to 19 year olds (66%) more likely to do so than the older 20 to 24 year olds (48%). The most common activities for teens were in education and research organizations, social services, sports and recreational activities. About 10% of 15 to 19 year olds volunteered in religious organizations.

COMPULSORY VOLUNTEERING IN ONTARIO?

In the province of Ontario in Canada, the recent requirement that Ontario high school students complete 40 hours of community service as part of the requirement for graduation provides an excellent opportunity for volunteering. Some students see this as a chore that they have to complete. There are also many students who have identified areas where they could be helpful and who spend hours trying to improve the conditions that they perceive as needing their assistance. All said, young people are in an ideal position to make major contributions in the area of volunteering and gain valuable experience in the process.

BARRIERS TO VOLUNTEERING

Many people see volunteering as something they can do, while others point to many barriers that prevent them from doing so. Here are some of the common barriers that are highlighted.

NO TIME – MUST WORK

When asked about barriers to volunteering, many young people both in Canada and the United States said they had limited time, because many of them had to work. Some also noted that they did not think they had any skills to contribute to volunteer work.

NO SKILLS TO OFFER

Those students who believe that they have no skills to offer would find on closer investigation into volunteering that in many instances, all that is needed is someone to listen, to be there, and to be a friend. This is something that most young people could contribute. In many instances, the best volunteer is a young person who could see things the way other young people do, and who could identify with the issues that others are experiencing. Sometimes, it takes one young person to interact with another to help in a crisis or to prevent one.

YOUNG PEOPLE HAVE SPECIAL SKILLS

Young people also have skills that they may not recognize as such. Being able to 'hang out', to listen to the same music as another, and to be helpful to an older person, are some of the things that young people can contribute. Besides, there are many young people with excellent skills that they never considered important, for example, being able to use a computer in a variety of ways that many older people cannot. Young people considering volunteering should make a list of the things they enjoy doing and things they know how to do. This could provide them with some direction as to where they can consider volunteering.

EACH PERSON HAS UNIQUE EXPERIENCES

The truth is that each person is unique, and each person has experiences that are unique to him or her. At times, there may be someone going through a situation that is very uncommon, but which another young person has already experienced. Think of the great impact the person with the previous experience could have on the person who is struggling with that same problem or issue!

IS IT SELFISHNESS NOT TO VOLUNTEER?

There are some people who would simply not be able to volunteer because of circumstances; but there are others who not believe in volunteering. One young person I taught told me in no uncertain terms that if he does anything for anyone, he has to be paid for his services. I found him particularly selfish, considering that at the time of our conversation I was actually volunteering in helping him to pass his last year of Math in high school.

But on reflection, I thought many of us live and think this way, although we do not put it into so many words. Being paid for services is something for which our society is programmed and which is considered a sign of success. But there is a far greater payment that comes from volunteering: knowing that one is helping someone who may not be able to afford to get the same help elsewhere. There is also the good feeling that one gets from helping others.

CAN'T TAKE GOOD FEELINGS TO THE BANK

One may argue that one can't take good feelings to the bank and this is very true. But there is good will that is produced by volunteering. Good will begets good will, and when one is helpful to others, invariably one receives help when one needs it; although it may come from somewhere else. Many people who volunteer speak about the advantages they experience in volunteering, to the extent that some volunteers believe they get more out of the experience than they contribute to others.

It is true that young people can get a part-time job and make money instead of spending time volunteering. But some young people may ask whether volunteering can be beneficial to them and what these benefits may be. Below are some of the benefits that are often highlighted.

PROMOTING FRIENDSHIP

Friendship is one advantage that is often mentioned. As pointed out earlier, some young people volunteer in order to spend time with their friends and to make new friends. Friendships are important and this is particularly the case for adolescents, where the peer group is often shown as more important than the family.

LEARNING NEW SKILLS

In many volunteer opportunities, young people learn new things, such as developing good social skills, excellent customer service methods, research skills, fundraising strategies, and marketing skills. Depending on the particular volunteer opportunities, young people may learn about the law and other disciplines.

LEARNING ABOUT ORGANIZATIONS AND CAREER PATHS

Young people have the opportunity to learn about the work that organizations are doing and about some of the ways these organizations are making a difference in the community. Many young people have been known to choose career paths, because their volunteering introduced them to new fields that they did not know existed.

GAINING GOOD JOB EXPERIENCE

Many young people find that the volunteer work they have done could be included on their resumes, and could give them credibility when they apply for a job. Also, most young people who volunteer find that this is an important way of building their resume because they are able to show future employers that they have work experience.

In many situations, young people who volunteer find out that the time may come when they are given a job with the very organization with which they volunteered, because their supervisors may have noted their good work ethics and performance. In fact, a survey in Ontario showed that 1 in every 2 youth volunteers between the ages of 15 and 24 noted that they volunteered to improve their opportunities for finding work.

LEARNING FIRSTHAND ABOUT PROFESSIONAL COMMITMENT

Some young people who aspire to follow professional careers, for example, medicine, social work, nursing, and business, among others, find that having volunteer experience in certain helping situations come in handy in showing their commitment to follow the particular professions.

Young people who aspire to a professional career would be well advised to include some volunteer work in their extracurricular activities, because this is something that weighs heavily in admissions to many colleges and universities in these disciplines. Many other disciplines are now requiring some volunteer experience as proof of the individual's commitment to working in the particular discipline.

REFERENCE LETTERS

Getting letters of reference is something that most young people will need sometime either for a job or to get into a college or university. A young person who has performed well in a volunteer position may find that getting a reference letter from a volunteer supervisor may go a long way to helping him or her obtain the job or achieve admission to their preferred college or university.

You may argue that in order to get into the best universities that you need to get good grades, and you know that you are an excellent student. While universities want the best scholars, they are also looking for something more.

They are looking for individuals that have leadership potential. This does not mean that you have to be a naturally bossy person, or someone who believes that in order to show leadership, you have to be strong and dominant, forcing others to do what you want them to do. Far from it. Universities are looking for students who are involved in their communities, who participate in various aspects of life, and who want to make a difference.

AN ACTUAL REQUIREMENT FOR UNIVERSITY APPLICATION

Many outstanding universities require students to send in application letters, stating why they want to attend the particular university. Many of these universities also request specific information as part of these applications. Here is one such request under the heading of "Leadership Profile" as part of a 2016 application:

"In the space provided, applicants must list extracurricular activities and/or community involvement that you participated in in the last 2 calendar years (i.e. 2014 and 2015). Include contact details for a referee that can validate your participation. Referees will be contacted directly by the university where necessary."

MUST PUT IN THE WORK

What this means is that you have to actually do the work and cannot depend on simply getting a reference letter from a family friend who is in some business or organization, saying that you are a fantastic worker. Gone are the days when you can depend on getting a letter from your uncle or family friend who is a professional vouching for your suitability to that profession.

A university may decide to follow up with your references directly, should they consider offering you a place in the upcoming school year. It also means that you cannot depend on old extracurricular activities. What you did five years ago may not be counted. What this also means is that some universities take this information seriously and consider it as part of your overall profile as a future student at their particular university.

Extracurricular activities and community involvement should therefore be important aspects in the lives of young people. Volunteering provides these opportunities to you.

BUT WHAT ABOUT VOLUNTEERING FOR ITS OWN SAKE?

However, if you are going to volunteer, think of the positive contribution you would make to others wherever you are placed. If you focus on what you could get out of volunteering, you would be shortchanging those you claim to want to help. You would also be shortchanging yourself as you would miss out on the benefits that accrue to those who give selflessly of themselves. You would never really know the true meaning of giving and those who are in the volunteer situation with you may see you as a selfish person.

CHAPTER 11 - FOOD FOR THOUGHT

TOPICS AND IDEAS FOR SELF-REFLECTION AND DISCUSSION

Self-Reflection

How do I feel about doing volunteer work?

What conditions have to be in place for me to volunteer?

Would I object if I had to do volunteer work in order to graduate?

If you were to volunteer, what are the best places to volunteer and why?

Group Discussion

What are the benefits for young people of volunteering?

Can you think of a volunteer activity that you can plan for your group, school or class? What do you see the activity as accomplishing?

CHAPTER 11 - REFERENCES AND FURTHER READING

Corporation for National & Community Service (2009, July). Volunteering in America Research Highlights. Retrieved from *http://www.fs.usda.gov/Internet/FSE_DOCUMEN TS/stelprdb5108473.pdf*

Hall, H. (2012). Half of American Teenagers volunteer largely because their friends do. The Chronicle of Philanthropy. Retrieved from *https://philanthropy.com/article/Half-of-American-Teenagers/155929*

University of Chicago, Institute of Politics (2016). Next Generation diplomacy: Leadership & diplomacy in the 21st century. Retrieved from *http://politics.uchicago.edu/pages/zeenat-rahman-seminar-series*

Vezina, M. & Crompton, S. (2012). Volunteering in Canada. Statistics Canada. Retrieved from *http://www.statcan.gc.ca/pub/11-008-x/2012001/article/11638-eng.htm*

LESSONS IN FINANCIAL RESPONSIBILITY

CONSUMERISM, A MAJOR CHALLENGE

Consumerism is seen as having two very distinct meanings. On the one hand, consumerism describes the movement to protect consumers from products that are inferior and of poor quality. On the other, consumerism is a theory based on the continuous spending of money and consumption of goods. These are considered activities associated with a way of life that is said to not only promote the economy, but also contribute to the wellbeing and happiness of society. Consumers are constantly bombarded through advertising with messages that give assurances that a measure of social and economic wellbeing is tightly bound up with being able to purchase things.

CASH NO LONGER KING

At one time, being able to buy things with cash was considered a sign of financial well-being. Today, things have changed. Convenience dictates being able to buy things without having cash on hand. With technology now making the marketplace more accessible to all, cash is no longer king. It is also not necessary to have the money available to buy. As one source explains, ". . . credit card companies, banks, and other financial institutions are inundating consumers with credit opportunities – the ability to apply for credit cards or pay off one card with another (Zucchi, October 11, 2019).

With a vast array of goods and services now available for purchase online and with the wide availability of credit, some consumers are getting themselves into serious financial trouble as they overconsume and push themselves into debt.

WHAT IS FINANCIAL LITERACY

Zucchi (October 11, 2019) describes financial literacy as the "confluence of financial, credit and debt management and the knowledge that is necessary to make financially responsible decisions – decisions that are integral to our everyday lives." It includes knowing how a checking account works, how credit works, and how to control debt. Other important elements of financial literacy that are missing in the education of many young people include knowing how to use a budget and how to live within it, how to buy a home or rent an apartment, pay for education, and possibly save for emergency.

FINANCIAL LITERACY IN DECLINE

At one time, it was customary for people to try to balance their bank accounts every month – checking their expenses through their cancelled checks and ensuring that their bank accounts were balanced. This is not so much the practice nowadays. With increased credit, people may not feel as much pressure as before to make sure that they have money in the bank. If they want something, they simply take out their credit card and get it right away. They would pay for their purchases later. The decline in financial literacy is serious for as Breitbach and Walstad (2016) point out, financial literacy is important for the economic wellbeing of all individuals, but particularly for young adults.

This is the case for young people, because it "is at these early years of their adult lives . . . they assume full responsibility for managing and directing their financial affairs" (Breitbach & Walstad, 2016). The decisions that young adults make at this time have implications for the rest of their lives.

OLDER GENERATIONS – NOT ALWAYS GOOD STEWARDS

As Phillip (October 15, 2014) points out, Americans are not good at managing debt and saving. "Analysts from the Federal Reserve of New York stated that as of December 31, 2013, total consumer indebtedness was $11.52 trillion . . . (a number that) is over $3 trillion higher than the GDP of China" (Phillip, October 15, 2014). Herman and colleagues (2015) also reveal that "[l]arge segments of the U.S. population have low levels of financial capability" (p. 1). In recognition of this deficit, young people must take steps to improve their financial literacy before it is too late.

YOUNGER GENERATIONS AND THE INTERNET AGE

With teenagers and young adults born during the age of the Internet, online shopping, ready use of credit cards and instant gratification are all characteristics of everyday living. The idea of balancing bank accounts or of financial literacy in general is foreign to some born during this era.

SOURCES OF INFORMATION

Sources of information on financial literacy are banks, credit unions, brokerage firms, insurance firms, credit card companies, mortgage companies, financial planners, and other financial service companies.

With all of these professionals available to provide financial information, many individuals, young and old, find the prospect of using this information daunting and sometimes confusing. Consumerism continues to thrive.

CONSUMERISM, FINANCIAL LITERACY AND YOUNG PEOPLE

This consumerism is seen as affecting young people to a great extent. As noted, "Consumerism has increasingly come to affect mundane and everyday aspects of young people's lives. . . . Instead of empowering with freedom of choice, consumer culture represents an entrapment, an endless quest of acquisition tied to identity" (McGregor, 2007). The general thinking is that many young people see their identity as expressed through the things that they buy and they continue to overconsume in an effort to improve their perception of their social standing.

WITHOUT FINANCIAL LITERACY – FINANCIAL DIFFICULTIES

But without financial literacy, people tend to overconsume and overspend and before long they find themselves in financial difficulties.

However, there are certain important lessons that young people must bear in mind as they think of becoming financially responsible.

How To Develop Financial Responsibility

There are several measures that you can take to develop financial responsibility. Here are some common ones below.

Live Within Your Means

It is important to learn to live within your means. This includes not buying things that you cannot afford because you see other people buying these things, or because the advertisements tell that these are items that the more popular people would use.

Budget, Budget, Budget

Based on your income, plan your expenses. Create a list of the necessary expenses you have on a monthly basis and of the usual sources of income you have for the same period. The objective here is to at least match your expenses to your income or to balance your account. This will prevent you from overspending on some unnecessary items and depleting your funds before you get to the essential expenses, like rent and utilities.

Consider Your Cash Flow

But even when your income is adequate to cover your expenses, make sure that you will receive the income before the payments are to be made. You can still find yourself in financial difficulty if when your bill comes due you do not have the funds in hand to cover the bill.

HAVE A SAVINGS ACCOUNT

Savings is often described as 'paying yourself first' (Smith, May 30, 2019). As this author explains, "Spending every dime that you earn is simply irresponsible unless you have a massive trust fund that is so flush with cash that you will never outlive the earnings". Other than this, a responsible financial approach is to think of what you earn and what you need, and trying to balance these off while keeping a little as savings.

One recommendation that I have seen in several works is setting a goal of saving 10% of your income.

BUT PAY OFF CREDIT CARD RATHER THAN SAVE

Another recommendation is to pay off your credit cards which may have interest rates as high as 20% or more before saving your money where you get interest rates as low as 2% and 3%. If you are saving money at 3% interest rate, while paying 20% on your credit cards, you a paying a 17% rate to have a savings account!

HAVE AN EMERGENCY FUND

Emergencies happen and these are situations that usually require you to pay right away or to have funds that could be applied, when these emergencies occur. One emergency that young people should be concerned about is a health emergency. Make sure you have an extra amount of funds that you can use when you are faced with an emergency. With health care not fully covered in the United States, as it is in Canada, people are required to carry private insurance to cover some of these unexpected health costs.

Some young people are covered under their parents' insurance. It is a good idea to find out if you are covered there or if you are in a work situation, where you are covered in case of illness.

The Affordable Care Act is considered a blessing by some, while others would like to see it repealed. As noted, while the goal of the Affordable Care Act's provisions (is) to move toward universal health insurance coverage, another goal of insurance coverage is to protect the financial consequences of poor health" (Campbell & Shore-Sheppard, July 2020, p. 16). The important thing to keep in mind is that in case of health emergencies, you should be prepared, either with extra funds on hand or with an insurance program to cover the expenses.

SMALL EVERYDAY EXPENSES CAN ADD UP

Watch out for your small everyday expenses, like your visits to Starbucks, the gas station, or the convenient store around the block where you pick up a coffee, a Coke, a hamburger, a newspaper, or a small item that you really don't need, but which you pick up out of habit. These small expenses could add up and take a bite out of your budget. As one author points out, "By cutting only $3 a day and investing it, a young adult can be a millionaire by retirement" (Kennon, January 5, 2018).

DISTINGUISH BETWEEN NECESSITIES AND LUXURIES

Teens and young adults must make a distinction between things that are necessities and those that are luxuries.

If you are a teen or young adult thinking of satisfying your transportation needs, you may find that it is practical to use public transportation.

But you may need a car to go to work as it may be inconvenient to use public transportation. You decide to get a practical car to take you to and from work. You see this as a necessity. But this car does not have to be top-of-the-line. However, if you decide to purchase a high-end car, you may find that you would have to pay much more than you can really afford.

STUDENT LOANS, CAR PAYMENTS AND CREDIT CARDS

These are expenses that many teens and young adults have to consider. An important concept that many young people overlook is the issue of cash flow. It is necessary to keep watch on when the money comes in and whether it is in time to cover the ongoing payments. As Kennon (January 5, 2018) explains, young people must realize that when they make a major purchase that it has an impact on their financial commitment and that this could impact their ongoing expenses. The availability of credit cards, though convenient at times, could have a tremendous impact on how young people spend.

UNDERSTAND CREDIT CARDS AND OTHER DEBT

Teens and young adults who have grown up in this Internet age are often blindsided by the ease of purchasing online and the easy access to credit. Even in setting up their first apartments, young people are often able to get credit from furniture, appliance and electronic stores, and some young consumers are even offered deals including zero-down financing and no payments for 12 months.

What many teens and young adults forget, or may not take into consideration, is that if nothing changes, things would very much be the same in the future as they are at the time of the purchases (Kennon, January 5, 2018).

If you do not have a job and do not have much of a prospect of getting one in the near future, this means that the debt you are incurring would be the debt you would have to repay in the near future, but only then with interest. This makes the item that you buy more expensive in the long run, as things would cost more than the purchase price (Smith, May 30, 2019). Also, there is the issue of repayment to consider.

When purchasing a car, remember to take the cost of insurance on the car into consideration. If you fail to do this, you could end up with a car that you could barely afford, and with no insurance. You may then have to look to your parents to help you cover costs to get your car up and running. (Smith, May 30, 2019).

CREDIT SCORES, BILL PAYMENTS AND INTEREST

Young people must pay attention to paying their bills on time. In the first place, if you pay your credit card bills late, you will incur interest on the total amount outstanding. If you pay the bill by the due date, you will only have to pay interest on the amount owing after your payment for that month is taken out.

Further, if you are frequently late, your credit score could suffer.

Although you may pay your bills every month, paying them late would have a negative impact on your credit score. It is important to understand that with a low credit score you may have difficulty not only holding on to your credit cards, but also getting credit to buy a home or even to rent an apartment. Paying your bills on time is therefore a necessary aspect of financial responsibility.

EXAMINE FINANCIAL SITUATION

Over time, examine your financial situation. Evaluate your earnings and your spending habits to make necessary adjustments to keep you financially responsible.

FORGO THE NEWEST GADGETS

Don't be tempted with the newest gadgets because advertisers tell you that the newest version of the product will be out in a month. For example, if your phone is still working well, then getting the newest phone will be really a luxury and not a necessity. If you are on a limited budget, it may make good sense to hold on to your existing phone because it is still serving you well.

CHOOSE REASONABLY-PRICED PRODUCTS

If you are on a limited budget, choose reasonably-priced products. Advertisers often provide celebrities with their products free of charge because advertisers know the power of these celebrities as "influencers" of average consumers. Yet, it is the average consumers, some with very limited incomes, who pay for these high-priced products. While having these new gadgets may be considered image-boosting, it could also be budget-breaking, causing financial upheaval.

CHOOSE YOUR COLLEGE WISELY

In many cases an undergraduate degree at a private college which is high-priced may not carry more weight academically than an undergraduate degree at a state university. Be aware of the value of the degree. What really matters is how you use this education.

CHOOSE YOUR CAREER PATH WISELY

Also, know what the required education is for the career you decide to follow. In some instances, what you may need is an internship or technical training, both of which may cost less than a university degree. It will also take less time to be qualified. Young people need to take into consideration that the world of work may not be as steady as it was during their parents' employment. As Peetz (2012) maintains, the future world of work seems to be becoming increasingly flexible, with the employment relationship changing, and with much work carried out by robots.

Young people will do well to look into the changes that are taking place in employment and the labour market, and decide how they could become more skilled in the new areas of employment that are emerging (Shockness, 2020).

NEW WAYS OF RECRUITMENT

In 2018, Kersten (February 15, 2018) reports that Toyota Motor Corp. in Story County, Iowa, was holding a "Parents' Night" and had plans to hold a couple others in order to introduce parents to their plant "to tour careers in toolmaking". Similarly, the Chamber of Commerce in Greenville, South Carolina, held a "Parents' Night" hosted by manufacturers with a similar aim in mind.

This is a recruitment strategy some employers are using in order to show that there are different routes to success besides college. Kersten (February 15, 2018) quotes the Wall Street Journal as stating: "In a time when many parents are worried about the cost of college, employers are spreading the message that teens with skills to fix machinery or design products are highly valued and that companies will even pay for them to attend school."

What this shows is that there are several ways of preparing for a career and young people need to consider the relative costs.

SPEAK TO CHILDREN ABOUT FINANCIAL RESPONSIBILITY

Parents must spend time speaking to their children about financial responsibility, and this should start very early in a child's life. But this does not happen often, as many parents are not financially literate themselves. Davies, Syed and Appleyard (2016) believe that schools can play an important role in teaching students how government and banks manage money and how these policies affect individuals. Financial literacy is therefore seen not only as personal responsibility but as a responsibility that schools should also share.

However, young people, who would be or who are already, young parents, should consider breaking the cycle of financial illiteracy, educate themselves on the subject, and so start off the next generation on the right track of embracing financial learning about money and banking. Starting young children on the idea of saving in a piggy bank, something that harks back to an earlier time, may not be such a bad idea.

READ POSITIVE BOOKS ON WEALTH CREATION

Young people who aspire to be wealthy or to learn more about financial responsibility should read positive books on the subject and on honest wealth creation. There are numerous books on the market which attempt to educate young people on how to make the most of their incomes and how to develop financial responsibility.

CHAPTER 12 - FOOD FOR THOUGHT

TOPICS AND IDEAS FOR SELF-REFLECTION AND DISCUSSION

Self Reflection

Based on the information provided, am I financially responsible?

Am I living within my means?

In what areas do I need to make changes to become financially responsible?

Do I use my credit card responsibly?

"How can I improve my situation and what steps should I take to achieve this?"

Group Discussion

Plan an activity with each individual undertaking to start a personal budget. Or members or students can be asked to create a budget for an individual or a family of 4, based on a household income of $60,000 or $80,000. Any other scenarios can be used.

After planning, group members or students can then discuss in a group setting how they budgeted for the individual or family, and can compare the significance of budgeting and what each individual or family accomplished. This will help build financial literacy for all group members or students.

CHAPTER 12 - REFERENCES AND FURTHER READING

Breitbach, E. & Walstad, W. B. (2016). Financial literacy and financial behavior among young adults in the United States. In Wuttke, E., Seigfried, J. & Schumann, S. (2016). Economic Competence and Financial Literacy of Young Adults. Verlag Barbara Budrich, 81-98.

Campbell, A. L. & Shore-Sheppard, L. (July 2020). The social, political, and economic effects of the Affordable Care Act: Introduction to the issue. The Russell Sage Journal of the Social Sciences, 6(2), 1-40

Davies, P., Syed, F.R. & Appleyard, L. (2016). Secondary school students' understanding of the financial system. In Wuttke, E., Seigfried, J. & Schumann, S. (2016). Economic Competence and Financial Literacy of Young Adults. Verlag Barbara Budrich, 41-62.

Greentumble (July 22, 2016). The Negative Effects of Consumerism. Available at https://greentumble.com/the-negative-effects-of-consumerism/

Herman, R., Hung, A. A., Burke, J., Carman, K. G., Clancy, N., Kaufman, J. H. & Wilson, K. (2015). *Development of a K-12 financial education curriculum assessment rubric*. Rand Corporation.

Hill, J. A. (April 2011). Endangered childhoods: How consumerism is impacting Child and Youth Identity. Media Culture & Society, 33(3), 347-362.

Kennon, J. (January 5, 2018). Teach your teen financial responsibility. The Balance. Available at https://www.thebalance.com/teach-your-teen-financial-responsibility-356152

Kersten, K. (February 15, 2018). How to reach high school students? Manufacturers try going straight to their parents. Center of the American Experiment. Available at https://www.americanexperiment.org/2018/02/reach-high-school-students-manufacturers-try-going-straight-parents/

Lake, R. (December 15, 2014). 23 Teenage consumer spending statistics that will shock you. Credit Donkey. Available at https://www.creditdonkey.com/teenage-consumer-spending-statistic.html

Loprest, P.., Spaulding, S., & Nightingale, D. S. (December 2019). Disconnected young adults: Increasing engagement and opportunity. The Russell Sage Foundation Journal of the Social Sciences, 5(5), 221-243.

O'Connor. A. (March 29, 2014). What scares you more: Giving your teenager the keys to your car or your credit card? Credit Donkey. Available at https://www.creditdonkey.com/teenagers.html

Peetz, D. (2012). Flexibility, the 'gig economy' and the employment relationship. In Peetz, D. (2012). The Realities and Futures of Work. ANU Press.

Phillip, K. (October 15, 2014). Teaching financial responsibility to our youth. Brothers on the Avenue. Available at https://brothersontheavenuellc.wordpress.com/201 4/10/15/teaching-financial-responsibility-to-our-youth/

Seefeldt, K. S. (June 2015). Constant consumption smoothing, limited investments, and few repayments: The role of debt in the financial lives of economically vulnerable families. Social Service Review, 89(2), 263-300.

Shockness, I. (September 5, 2020). Becoming equipped for jobs in the 21st century. Successful Youth Living Blog. Available at https://www.successfulyouthlivingblog.com/2020/0 9/05/becoming-equipped-for-jobs-in-the-21st-century/

Smith, L. (May 30, 2019). The basics of financial responsibility. Investopedia. Available at https://www.investopedia.com/articles/pf/09/finan cial-responsibility.asp

Straw, T., Lueck, S. & Aron-Dine, A. (2020). Congress should bolster ACA marketplace coverage amid COVID-19: Marketplaces can do even more to protect people from health and economic hardship. Center on Budget and Policy Priorities.

USA Gov. (August 19, 2020). Credit Reports and Scores. Available at https://www.usa.gov/credit-reports#item-213816

Zucchi, K. (October 11, 2009). Why financial literacy is so important. Investopedia. Available at https://www.investopedia.com/articles/investing/100615/why-financial-literacy-and-education-so-important.asp

TAKING RESPONSIBILITY FOR GETTING ALONG –DEALING WITH RACISM

WHY WRITE ABOUT RACISM?

When we speak about 'racism', we often see it as a dirty word that many people would rather not hear or speak about. While there are many people who speak about experiencing racism in certain encounters, there are others pointing out that there is no racism intended in such encounters and that the charge of racism is false. But it is important to understand that racism is not in the intent, but in the effect (Dei, 1996A & 1996B). Often, a person who has been called a racist would point out, "I am not a racist; I did nothing wrong," while the person who was impacted by the action continues to make a charge of racism. What is happening here? Are these two individuals not dealing with the same facts?

THREE IMPORTANT POINTS ABOUT RACISM

There are three important points that you should consider when speaking about racism: know what you are speaking about, identify the act of racism, and consider what racism is.

KNOW WHAT YOU ARE SPEAKING ABOUT

First, when the term 'racism' is used, know what you are speaking about. If you feel you are a victim of racism, express specifically the feeling that you experienced and the action that caused you to feel that way. If you are accused of racism, don't go on the defensive. Find out what you did that caused the other person to call you a racist. Consider the action that caused you to be accused of racism. Remember, racism is not in the intent, but in the effect. It is not what you intended to do, but how your actions made the other person feel.

IDENTIFY THE ACT

Secondly, if you feel you are the victim of racism, identify the act as racism, and not call the person a racist. If you call the person a racist, which has a lot of baggage associated with it, that person would try to defend himself or herself by saying that he or she is not a racist. Nothing is gained here. It is better to say to the person that he or she has carried out an act that is racist or that smacks of racism, even though you feel like hurting the person by calling him or her a racist. But by referring to the act as racist, you are giving that person the opportunity to see his or her behaviour as something that can be changed. If you call the person a racist, then you leave no opportunity for the person to change. Being a racist then becomes part of that person's identity and is seen as permanent.

Have you been accused of being a racist? If so, realize that it is possible that your actions may have had a racist effect, one of which you were not aware.

Think about it. The person who is claiming racism is not irrational or crazy, so that there must be something in what you said or did that prompted that person to think the way he or she did. Even if you are tempted to say that the particular person who called you a racist is crazy, think about it.

All those individuals who say that they are the victims of racism cannot be all crazy. You have to admit that there are certain acts that have the effect of racism.

CONSIDER WHAT RACISM IS

Thirdly, whether victim or accused, you must consider what racism is. Basically, it is the "belief that race accounts for differences in human character or ability and that a particular race is superior to others." This has been shown to be a wrong assumption. This belief could be manifested in different ways in our society and this is the source of the conflict between those who claim they are victims of racism and those who claim that they did nothing racist. But racism is a false belief that is highly intertwined in all aspects of our lives, and so manifests itself in its many forms. As Davis (2010) points out: "The deep roots of racism are anchored in the false belief that one race or culture is superior" (p. 45). This is a false belief that must be acknowledged to be false, and every effort should be made to eradicate it. It is incumbent on those who experience it and those who are accused of perpetrating it to set out to get rid of it.

GETTING RID OF RACISM

It's not so easy, but it is worth the try. As an intelligent young person in the 21st century, you are in a good place in history to get rid of racism once and for all. It then becomes your responsibility to stamp it out at every instant. This means that those who are often the victims of racism must join forces with those who are often accused of racism to find racism wherever it appears, to acknowledge that it exists in various forms, and to remove it. This means that the two groups should unite against the common enemy of racism that threatens to destroy our civilization.

"ONENESS OF HUMANKIND"

Davis (2010) encourages us to think of the "Oneness of Humankind", that sees us united as one species, unique in our imagination, thought, comprehension and memory (p. 45).

TAKE-AWAY MESSAGE

"Healing racism entails a tremendous amount of personal reflection. All (of us) have been affected by racism, but each of us from every "race" and culture can heal" (Davis, 2010, p. 45). It is important to recognize that there are different forms of racism, and these must be understood and acknowledged if they are all to be addressed and eradicated.

POLICIES ARE URGENTLY NEEDED

While all of these statements represent steps that all individuals in the society can take to tackle racism, various government institutions must introduce policies to bring about change. As one observer commented: "Law enforcement should subject white racist organizations to the same surveillance and scrutiny as groups devoted to jihad. Governments at all levels should enforce fair housing and employment laws as vigorously as they enforce the Patriot Act. Police departments and court systems must be compelled to administer justice equally —with African Americans, too, considered innocent until proven guilty" (Robinson, 2015).

Some police departments are already recognizing that there is racism within their forces and some are already taking action to change things. But there must be political will to make changes and not an attempt to deny that racist actions do take place within their ranks. Greater awareness and efforts on the part of all government departments are needed to genuinely and honestly confront the issue of racism and try to eradicate it at every turn.

Also, it is when concrete steps are taken to remove inequities in society that the foundation would be laid for ending racism. Hate groups and ultra conservative white supremacist groups that speak hatred should also be exposed and curbed, and not be protected under free speech laws. These groups should be exposed as violating laws regarding life, liberty and the pursuit of happiness for all when they take racist actions. These are values considered important in western society.

END SUSPICIONS TO END RACISM

One important factor that must be stressed is that suspicion breeds racism. There is no room for suspicion among groups in society. When some police officers suspect that African American youths are out to get the police, and when some African American youths suspect that the police are out to get them, a serious situation develops. What is needed is a better understanding on the part of each group of the fears each group experiences. Some police officers and some African American youths need not see each other as the enemy and should not harbour hostility and fear.

If African American youths did not fear police, they would not have to be running away from them and get shot. Also, if some police officers did not fear African American youths and did not see them as their enemy, even when these youths are running away, they would not be motivated to shoot them.

RECONCILIATION

What is needed to start the process of healing racial tension is reconciliation. Bishop Tutu, in a speech several years ago, explained about a meeting he witnessed between police officers that were responsible for shooting a Black youth in the townships in South Africa and the family members and the community from which this young man had come. Bishop Tutu said that the expectation was that there would have been a physical confrontation between police and community members, and tempers flared as the two groups came together.

But just then, one police officer acknowledged that he was one of the police officers that had fired the shot that had killed the young man, and he expressed his deepest apology about doing so. Bishop Tutu said that the simple but meaningful words that the police officer had muttered, "I am sorry", had changed the whole tone of the meeting. These words brought about the forgiveness from the crowd that was formerly angry enough to come to blows with police.

If this simple act could have brought about forgiveness and reconciliation in a country like South Africa that was wracked with apartheid at the time, why can't much more be accomplished in the United States and other Western countries that preach democracy? If people of different ethnicities and races would join together to end racism, if they would try to get to know each other better, then there is a good chance that racism could be dealt a deadly blow.

If all concerned would put aside false pride and think of each other as what we are, simply human beings wanting a good life, then we would have a good chance of putting away our hatreds, suspicions, and fears, and of dealing with each other transparently and honestly. Then, we will be able to say to each other, "I am sorry", or "I have forgiven you", and genuinely mean it. Each side would have the capacity to accept and believe what the other side says. It is in an environment of reconciliation that we will see racism uprooted and destroyed.

CHAPTER 13 - FOOD FOR THOUGHT

TOPICS AND IDEAS FOR SELF-REFLECTION AND DISCUSSION

Self-Reflection

How has racism affected me or still affects me?

In what way? How did you feel? What do I do to deal with racism?

Group Discussion

What do you think about racism? Do you think racism affects all people in a society, despite their race, ethnicity, or national origin?

How many types of racism are you aware of, and how many have you seen at work in the society?

What are some ways of addressing racism in society?

Chapter 13 - References and Further Reading

Crenshaw, W., Gotanda, N., Feller, G. & Thomas, K. (1995). (Eds.), *Critical Race Theory: The Key Writings that formed the movement.* New York: The New Press.

Davis, S. E. (2010). The Oneness of Humankind: Healing Racism Today. *Reclaiming Children and Youth.* Winter, 18(4), 44-47

Dei, G. J. Sefa, (1996A). *Anti-Racism Education: Theory and Practice.* Halifax, Nova Scotia: Fernwood Publishers.

Dei, G. J. Sefa (1996B). Critical perspectives in antiracism: An introduction. *The Canadian Review of Sociology and Anthropology,* 33(3), 247-267.

Henry, F., Tator, C., Mattis, W. & Rees, T. (1998). *The Color of Democracy: Racism in Canadian Society.* Toronto: Nelson Canada.

Robinson, E. (June 22, 2015). American will only end racism when it stops being racist. Washington Post Retrieved from *https://www.washingtonpost.com/opinions/the-roots-of-racism/2015/06/22/24e61d56-1909-11e5-bd7f-4611a60dd8e5_story.html*

Shockness, I. (2020). Respect is Only Human: A Response to Disrespect and Implicit Bias. Toronto: Vanquest Publishing. Available at https://www.amazon.com/dp/1775009483

THE DIFFERENT FORMS OF RACISM

DIFFERENT FORMS OF RACISM

It is important to recognize that there are different forms of racism, and these must be understood if they are all to be addressed and eradicated.

Generally, when we think of racism, the image that comes to mind is that of one person not liking another person because of his or her race, and of discriminating against or of denying access to that person of different resources because of that person's race. However, there are other forms of racism that may be less obvious, but more destructive.

The different forms of racism are individual racism, everyday racism, institutional or systemic racism, and cultural and ideological racism (Henry, Tator, Mattis & Rees, 1998). Scheurich and Young (1997) identify individual or personal racism, institutional racism and societal racism.

INDIVIDUAL OR PERSONAL RACISM

Individual or personal racism can be overt, but it can also be covert or hidden. Scheurich and Young (1997) describe individual racism as "a public, conscious and intended act by a person or persons of one race with the intent of doing damage to a person or persons of another race chiefly because of the race of that second person or persons". These researchers describe covert racism as similar to overt racism, except that the former is not public, and efforts are usually made to hide the true nature of racism.

In today's society, people would seldom declare publicly that they have a personal dislike for another person based primarily on the other person's race or ethnicity, except those hate groups that make this their agenda. Part of the reason for this is that many people have become sophisticated enough to realize that people are the same under the skin. However, many people may still dislike people of other ethnic or racial groups, but may not even admit this to themselves. Most people want to be thought of as not holding ethnic or racial biases.

Yet, there are still instances of covert personal racism. Henry, Tator, Mattis and Rees (1998) note: "Individual racism has been defined as the attitude, belief, or opinion that one's own racial group has superior values, customs and norms and, conversely, that other racial groups possess inferior traits and attributes". These authors argue, though, that having these attitudes, beliefs, or opinions, does not necessarily lead to discriminatory behaviour. On this basis, they believe that there is a need to look to other forms of racism. "It is therefore important to move the conception of racism beyond a focus on interpersonal animosity" (Henry, Tator, Mattis and Rees, 1998). **Individual or personal racism is the racism we often think about when the term 'racism' is used.**

EVERYDAY RACISM

Speaking about everyday racism, Henry, Tator, Mattis and Rees (1998) point out that it "involves the many and sometimes small ways in which racism is experienced by people of color in their interactions with the dominant White group. It expresses itself in glances, gestures, forms of speech and physical movements. Sometimes, it is not even consciously experienced by its perpetrators, but it is immediately and painfully felt by its victims – the empty seat next to a person of color, which is the last to be occupied in a crowded bus, the slight movement away from a person of color in an elevator . . . and the ubiquitous question to a person of color born in the United States or Canada, "Where did you come from?"" Everyday racism manifests itself in many ways that are easily identifiable by people who are the victims of this form of racism.

Everyday racism is the racism that manifests itself when a store clerk follows a Black person or person of color around in a store, probably with the anticipation that the Black person or person of color may steal, a thinking that comes out of a stereotype. I found a video some time ago that also revealed how many people of color are accused of stealing or doing a criminal act simply because of the stereotypes concerning people of color.

The point made in this video is that it is not enough to accuse someone. It is important to consider an individual innocent until that individual can be proven guilty. But what was interesting in the video was the race of the accuser and the race of the accused. Look at it here:

http://www.humanrights.com/what-are-human-rights/videos/innocent-till-proven-guilty.html

EXAMPLES OF EVERYDAY RACISM

It is also everyday racism that is evident when a Black person is speaking to a store clerk, and a White customer comes up and the clerk immediately turns away to help the White customer, leaving the Black customer standing unattended. On the other hand, when a Black customer comes up to a White clerk who is attending to a White customer and may wish to ask a very short question, such as a direction to a department, the White clerk may either ignore the question, or may emphatically let the Black customer know that the clerk is attending to another customer and therefore cannot help the Black customer at the time. The time spent informing the Black customer of this could have been spent pointing the Black customer in the direction of the appropriate department. This happens very frequently, more frequently than one may imagine! In an informal focus group two years ago, many non-White parents reported being treated differently than White parents in their meeting with some White teachers on parent/teacher night (Shockness, 2003).

In another example of everyday racism, a well-meaning White woman had stopped at a home in a nice neighborhood, where she was having car troubles. In trying to move her car, she had also accidentally hit a cat. As she knocked at the door to enquire whether the cat had belonged to that household, a Black woman went to the door. The woman who had hit the cat asked politely, "May I see the lady of the house?" The Black woman said "Yes"? and waited to hear what the woman at the door wanted. But the White woman again repeated her request to see the lady of the house.

The Black woman again replied, "Yes," and waited to hear what the woman had to say. Realizing that the woman at the door was not going to say what she wanted and also realizing the embarrassing situation that was unfolding, the Black woman closed the door and then returned, "Yes, you wanted to see me?"

It was not until then that it had dawned on the White woman at the door that the Black woman that had answered the door was also the owner of the home. At that point, very embarrassed the White woman awkwardly tried to explain her error. As it stood, this was everyday racism, as the White woman, from stereotypes, did not expect a Black woman to be "the woman of the house" in the particular middle upper-class neighborhood. According to the Black woman who experienced this, "This is not the worst thing that has happened to me." This is just another case of microaggression that some people belonging to different ethnic groups experience on a daily basis (Shockness, 2020).

INSTITUTIONAL RACISM

Another kind of racism that Scheurich and Young (1997) spoke about is institutional racism. These authors describe this form of racism as existing "when institutions or organizations, including educational ones, have standard operating procedures (intended or unintended) that hurt members of one or more races in relation to members of the dominant race" (Scheurich and Young, 1997). Institutional racism also takes place when organizations have "cultures, rules, habits, or symbols" that cause members of other groups to experience hurt or to see a bias against them.

Henry, Tator, Mattis and Rees (1998) point out: "Institutional racism is manifested in the policies, practices, and procedures of various institutions, which may, directly or indirectly, consciously or unwittingly, promote, sustain, or entrench differential advantage or privilege for people of certain races."

Like individuals, institutions could act in racist ways, either overtly or inherently. Policies and procedures can be overtly racist, such as excluding people of color from services, but it is possible that institutions can adopt policies that do not specifically exclude certain groups, but the policies could nevertheless have the effect of excluding these groups.

However, institutions are made up of people, and people make decisions. One may take the position that it takes racist people to make up these policies in institutions that have inherently racist effects. This is not generally the case. Lopez (2000) points out that institutional racism "explains organizational activity that systematically harms minority groups even though the decision-making individuals lack any conscious discriminatory intent." It is significant, though, to bear in mind that racism resides not in the intent but in the effect.

Lopez (2000) believes that institutional racism arises because individuals in organizations have developed certain ways of thinking and of doing things that become automatic in decision-making. In other words, decision-making follows certain rules and scripts and individuals no longer use conscious thought in analyzing the way decisions are made. They simply follow the script and rules, and make their decisions. Even when they have to think, they are used to thinking in certain prescribed ways that appear 'natural'. In other words, their thinking and actions smack of racism.

EXAMPLES OF INSTITUTIONAL RACISM

Examples of institutional racism can be seen in organizations that have rules or practices that traditionally and automatically exclude certain groups, or that deal with issues that are pertinent to some groups and not others. It is also seen in organizations that refuse to address issues that are pertinent to some groups, because these groups may not be thought of as possessing economic and/or political power. Institutional racism occurs when responsible members of organizations do not take measures to change existing inequities, or when they do not see reason for change.

It also persists when people in policy-making positions overlook complaints of inherently racist policies by taking the position that they cannot help the results of the policies, because this is the way things are, or that they are only going by the rules.

In our society, institutional racism is beginning to be given greater consideration, although there is a great deal of work still to be done.

SOCIETAL RACISM/CULTURAL AND IDEOLOGICAL RACISM

Another kind of racism is societal racism (Scheurich and Young, 1997). Henry, Tator, Mattis & Rees (1998) refer to this kind of racism as cultural and ideological racism. This type of racism exists in the society as a whole and is evident "when prevailing societal and cultural assumptions, norms, concepts, habits, expectations . . . favor one race over one or more other races" (Scheurich and Young, 1997).

Henry, Tator, Mattis and Rees (1998), drawing on the work of another scholar, notes:

"Essed (1990) argues that cultural racism precedes other forms of racism in society. It is reflected in everyday language – "whiteness" is associated with overwhelming positive connotations, while "blackness," in Roget's Thesaurus, has no fewer than sixty distinctively negative synonyms, twenty of which are related to race. Cultural racism is reflected in the images generated by the mass media (racial minorities are often portrayed as problems), and by the arts (literature, poetry, and visual art often deal in stereotypes). It is also manifested in some religious doctrines, ideologies, and practices."

An example of cultural racism that was pointed out by one Black woman was a recent advertisement by a well-known manufacturer of tissue paper. The message behind the advertisement was that regardless of the situation, their tissue is available to wipe away the tears. The advertisement was placed on all the subway stations, buses and bus shelters. It consisted of three panels.

On one panel, there was a picture of a small White boy displaying two situations: in one case, he was crying because he did not like carrots or some other vegetable and on the other he was crying because he may have been afraid. On another panel, there was a picture of a White man: in one case, he seemed to have an allergy, and in the other he may have needed to wipe his eyes. The tissue came in handy for the people on both of these panels, as they could have used the tissue to wipe their eyes, if needed.

In the third panel, there was a picture of a Black woman with an extremely distressed look on her face, where she would have wiped her tears with the tissue. In one case, the caption was basically that her son had left home. The caption for the second incident was that her son had moved back home. She was crying in both of these cases.

When comparing the incidents in the two panels mentioned above for the small boy and the man with the incidents in the panel with the Black woman, what becomes apparent is that in the first two panels mentioned, the scenarios were about things and/or situations that were not serious. In the third panel with the Black woman, from her distressed appearance the incidents involved her son and were serious.

The message that was interpreted by some is that her son caused her sorrow, whether he had left home or returned. This was a further negative image of the Black male in our society, namely, the cause of his mother's pain. These are some of the messages that people from marginalized groups are faced with as examples of cultural racism.

Ideological racism is evident, for while our society speaks very highly of the values of democracy, many forms of racism still exist within it. This is what Henry, Tator et al. (1998) describe as 'democratic racism'.

Ideological racism is evident, for while our society speaks very highly of the values of democracy, many forms of racism still exist within it. This is what Henry, Tator, Mattis and Rees (1998) describe as 'democratic racism'.

EXAMPLES OF INSTITUTIONAL RACISM

This racism (societal, cultural, and ideological) is also based on the stereotypes that are perpetuated through the media. This is evident in the way reports are made, the descriptions that are provided, and the images that are projected. Even when insinuations are made, this is often sufficient to maintain stereotypes. Through jokes, people perpetuate these stereotypes. Novelists, filmmakers, and writers attempt to make their work as realistic as possible, and often resort to using stereotypes that have been tested and tried over time, and that convey the messages they want. The result is that novels, films, and other creative work often hold on to stereotypes long after people have started discarding them. This helps to reinforce these old stereotypes and hurt the cause of people of particular ethnicities and races.

Several racial and ethnic groups suffer from societal racism. For example, First Nations people and Blacks are often depicted in negative light, with the negative images being rampant in articles, literature, films, and other media. There are numerous instances where societal racism is accepted as the norm. Images of poverty, illiteracy, and crime are often linked automatically with race and ethnicity, and perpetuate the idea of inferiority. Immigrants from certain countries are also linked in this way.

These are images that are damaging, particularly to the young people of the racial and ethnic groups that are negatively portrayed. Societal racism may be said to receive the least amount of attention, despite the fact that it is so pervasive and so damaging.

CHAPTER 14 - FOOD FOR THOUGHT

TOPICS AND IDEAS FOR SELF-REFLECTION AND DISCUSSION

Self-Reflection

What actions do I take that unwittingly contributes to racism?

Do I laugh at ethnic jokes?

Discussion

If you are in a group where people are telling ethnic jokes, how would you respond?

If you see an advertisement that stereotypes people of different ethnic groups, what action can you take to show disapproval of this stereotyping?

CHAPTER 14 - REFERENCES AND FURTHER READING

Henry, F., Tator, C., Mattis, W. & Rees, T. (1998). *The Color of Democracy: Racism in Canadian Society.* Toronto: Nelson Canada.

Huff, D. (1997). To Live Heroically: Institutional *Racism and American Indian Education.* New York: State University of New York Press.

Li, Z. (1994). Structural and psychological dimensions of racism: towards an alternative perspective. *Canadian Ethnic Studies, 26*(3), 122-134.

Lopez, I. F. H. (2000). Institutional Racism:Judicial conduct and a new theory of racial discrimination. *The Yale Law Journal, 109*(6), 1717-1884.

Nile, L. N. & Straton, J. C. (2003). Beyond Guilt: How to Deal with Societal Racism. *Multicultural Education, 10*(4), 2-6.

Shockness, I. (2020). Respect is Only Human: A Response to Disrespect and Implicit Bias. Toronto: Vanquest Publishing. Available at https://www.amazon.com/dp/1775009483

CHAPTER 15

ENDING RACISM: BE PART OF THE SOLUTION NOT THE PROBLEM

A CHALLENGE FOR YOUTHS

A society without racism would be a society that could make it possible for most people within that society to excel. If most people excel, then the society would be better off, economically, creatively, spiritually, emotionally, politically, and ethically. If every individual were to take whatever measures he or she can to deal with racism, little by little minds could be changed and the new generations that are coming would not be poisoned or even tainted with the venom of racism.

UNDERSTANDING RACISM

If you are a young person, regardless of your race or ethnicity, racism is something you must endeavour to understand, for it is in understanding it that you can stamp it out. If you belong to a privileged group in society, do not be fooled into thinking that racism is not your concern or problem, or not in your interest. A nation's wealth is eroded when part of that nation does not have the opportunity to reach its potential, and everyone in that nation is impoverished in the process.

DOING WHAT YOU CAN TO END RACISM

If you are a young person who belongs to a marginalized group within the society, see it as your mission to do everything possible in your power to bring about change. It does not make sense to become frustrated or lament the fact that social justice is often in such short supply. When you become frustrated, there is one of two ways you may go. You may become destructive of the forces you believe prevent you from moving forward or from realizing your dream of personal fulfillment. **This is counter-productive, for you could be only pushing yourself further back. Violence does not solve problems. It only creates more.**

BE CREATIVE TO SURMOUNT PROBLEMS

The other choice is to be creative, and find ways of surmounting the difficulties that you encounter. Think of ways of eliminating those difficulties and of making the way easier for yourself and those coming behind. This often involves bringing injustices to the attention of those who have the power to make changes, and showing them the urgency in making these necessary changes. This also involves engaging the political process in a meaningful way. It could involve voting for the particular candidate or party that recognizes the need for these changes, working as a volunteer for such a candidate or party, or running for office yourself and campaigning on a platform that supports these changes. The various political parties have youth wings or chapters, which would be only too happy to welcome you to their ranks! Check out the political platforms and belief systems of the political parties, and choose the one that best supports your cause. If none supports your cause, then make it your business to bring your issue to the forefront where it could attract the attention of those who want your support, and who would be willing to work for your support. Get involved politically and promote ways of ending racism, especially in its subtler forms.

BE BRAVE AND BOLD

Over the years, our society has made steps forward in eliminating some of the more blatant forms of racism, and it took individuals who were brave enough to stand up and condemn those blatant forms of racism. Following the same tradition of tackling racism requires brave individuals, brave young people, who can recognize racism in its many manifestations and disguises, and who are willing to take a stand to eliminate these wherever, and whenever, possible.

SOME SUGGESTIONS FOR STAMPING OUT RACISM

- Don't judge individuals on the basis of group stereotypes.
- Don't treat people in certain ways, because of stereotypes.
- Challenge stereotypes wherever you encounter them.
- Learn about different cultures. Join groups where you have an opportunity to meet people from different cultures and form friendships.
- Be sensitive to the feelings of people from other cultural groups. They are human and have the same feelings you do.
- Don't assume that people from other cultural groups can't see or understand your motives or actions. Racist actions are very obvious to those who are subjected to them.

- Regardless of your ethnic or racial background, don't limit yourself. Aspire to the greatest possible heights you can achieve. Don't let anyone tell you that you can't achieve something because of your race or ethnicity!
- Read and learn about different cultures.
- Be respectful of difference.
- Be critical readers and thinkers. Question images and ideas that support racism, and be aware that many of these images and ideas appear in the media – advertising, movies, and articles, for example. They may appear in the use of a word, a gesture, a pose, or a symbol.
- Denounce media that promote hatred about certain groups.
- Call out the media when they promote negative images of different groups.
- Be conscious of advertising that consistently presents certain groups as poverty-stricken or in negative light.
- Boycott media that masquerade as mainstream, while promoting racial hatred.
- Denounce political leaders and candidates who speak hatred about particular ethnic or racial groups.
- Don't believe everything you hear.
- Don't tell racist jokes, regardless of how harmless they may appear and even if it is about your own ethnic or racial group.
- Most importantly, be proud of your heritage, but don't promote it as being better than others.

- Point out practices in institutions that are unfair to individuals of different ethnic groups and try to bring about changes, even if your group is not one of those being discriminated against.
- Point out practices in the society that discriminate against certain groups.
- Challenge your fraternity or sorority brothers and sisters who may try to promote your groups by using racist chants and epithets to taunt members of organizations that cater to other cultural groups.
- Request that universities not only suspend minor privileges, but take comprehensive action against fraternities and sororities that support racist practices, that universities send a tough message to members that such action will not be tolerated. Threat of disbanding of such organizations or suspending operations for a year or more may appear severe, but could be an important action taken by universities to discourage racism.
- As a creator of artistic works, such as videos, novels, paintings, films, etc., avoid choosing the low road and stop using stereotypes to enhance credibility and to move your story forward.

- Note practices in your daily activities that suggest some people are more important than others, because of the racial or cultural groups to which they belong. For example, as a clerk, do not ignore the customer from a minority group to attend to a customer from a privileged group. Or as a teacher, do not overlook the parent of a child of a visible minority group in order to spend extra time with the parent of a child from a privileged group, and do not ignore the child in your class who is a recent immigrant or make that child feel that he or she does not belong.

- Add your own ideas as to how you can have a positive impact in putting an end to racist practices!!

INDIVIDUAL EFFORT AND POLITICAL WILL

Racism can be eliminated, but it will take individual effort and commitment, and real political will and ingenuity to bring this about. Young people have the power to demand what they want. This demand does not have to involve violence. By choosing where to spend your money, which politicians to support, and which products to purchase or boycott, young people could subtly influence the critical decisions that are in their interest and that need to be made. At a time when we have invented the Internet, established a station on the moon, and have discovered several new planets, it seems hopeful to think that with the same intelligence we can bring an end to racism. If we look closely, racism is at the root of all the trouble we have in the world today, whether we acknowledge this or not. Making racism history promises to give us a better world for this and future generations.

CHAPTER 15 - FOOD FOR THOUGHT

TOPICS AND IDEAS FOR SELF-REFLECTION AND DISCUSSION

Self-Reflection

Do you think the end of racism would be good for society? Why?

Group Discussion

What are measures that individuals and groups could undertake to bring about an end to racism?

CHAPTER 15 - REFERENCES AND FURTHER READING

James, C. E. (1995). *Seeing ourselves: Exploring race, ethnicity and culture.* Toronto: Thomson

James, C. E. (2001). "Multiculturalism, Diversity, and Education in the Canadian Context: The Search for an Inclusive Pedagogy," in C. A. Grant and J. L. Lei (Eds.), *Global Constructions of Multicultural Education: Theories and Realities.* Hillsdale, New Jersey: Erlbaum Associates.

James, C.E. & Brathwaite, K. S. (1996). The Education of African Canadians: Issues, contexts, and expectations. In C.E. James & Brathwaite, K. S. (Eds.), *Educating African Canadians.* Toronto: Our Schools/Our Selves, James Lorimer.

Ladson-Billings, G. & Tate, W. F. (1995). Toward a critical race theory in education. *Teachers College Record. 97*(1), 47-68.

Scheurich, J. & Young, M. (1997). Coloring Epistemologies: Are the Research Epistemologies Racially Based? *Educational Researcher,* 26(1).

Shockness, I. (2003). Findings of an Informal Focus Group.

Tatum, B. D. (1992). Talking about Race, Learning about Racism: The Application of Racial Identity Development Theory in the Classroom. *Harvard Educational Review.* 62(1).

Utsey, S. O., Ponterotto, J. G. & Reynolds, A. L. (2000). "Racial discrimination, coping, life satisfaction, and self-esteem among African Americans," *Journal of Counseling and Development*, 78(1), 72-80.

Vickers, J. (reviewer). Marchak, M. P. (1997). "Racism, sexism, and the university: the political science affair at the University of British Columbia. *Journal of Canadian Studies*, 32(2).

Shockness, I. (2020). Respect is Only Human: A Response to Disrespect and Implicit Bias. Toronto: Vanquest Publishing. Available at https://www.amazon.com/dp/1775009483

CHAPTER 16

TAKING RESPONSIBILITY TO BE A LEADER

Leadership is often thought of as a position that an individual holds. But the truth is, everyone can be a leader by choosing to do what needs to be done, and not waiting for someone else to step up and do it.

TAKING LEADERSHIP IN THE WORKPLACE

Taking responsibility to be a leader can be in a workplace, where one needs to take responsibility to help get something done, or where any employee can do that task. In situations like these, each employee may look to the other one to undertake the task. Since no one steps up, the task either remains undone, or someone is eventually told to do it, usually to that person's chagrin. This is not leadership, but shirking of responsibility.

Young people can take on the mantle of leadership if they work in a company or in a volunteer position where they notice that something is not working, and call attention to this situation. Or they may observe that something could be improved, and they could either mention it to someone who has the authority to make changes, or they could undertake to make the change, if this is within their authority. Young people can serve as leaders in suggesting improvement or taking responsibility for introducing improvement.

This is an approach young people can use in various situations. Using this approach can lead young people to develop many of the characteristics of leadership that would help in all aspects of their lives.

However, there are times when something just needs to be done, and you may be the only person on site that can do it. You have the choice to assess the situation and take on the leadership role to get this task done.

WHAT LEADERSHIP IS NOT

One of the responsibilities of a leader is to be a good example to others. Unfortunately, in today's society, many adults see leadership as a way of bossing others around. They believe that because they have the power to tell others what to do, that they should be rude about it. However, many leaders do not choose to tell others what to do, but rather join with others to decide what should be done. Leaders that make followers part of the decision-making process are usually the most effective leaders, because they allow followers to take ownership of decisions made. These decisions are often the most effective and most long-lasting.

Unfortunately, today, we find that many who aspire to be leaders see leadership as coming from a position of strength, with strength signifying brute force. In political quarters, leadership is sometimes seen as crushing other nations, dominating them, and depriving them of opportunities.

Leadership is also seen as preventing others from having the same opportunities we have by taking as much as we can for ourselves, knowing that when we take, they lose.

Political leadership today is seen as threats of war and threats of violence, and this is seen in well developed countries as well as from those struggling for global recognition. In economic terms, leadership is often seen as working for one's interest only, oblivious to the many people around who are being fleeced to provide wealth for the already wealthy. In short, leadership today is often seen as being insensitive to the needs of others and striving only for one's aggrandizement. This is seen as boasting about one's power and wealth, and being rude and arrogant about it.

LEADERSHIP IS ABOUT DIPLOMACY

But this is not what leadership is about. Leadership is about diplomacy, which in recent months seems to have become a dirty word. Those who aspire to leadership and who see diplomacy as politically incorrectness violate all standards of decorum and decency and miss the mark of being a leader.

WHAT IS DIPLOMACY?

What is diplomacy? As Bo Bennett, an American businessperson, observes, "Diplomacy is more than saying or doing the right things at the right time; it is avoiding saying or doing the wrong things at any time." Leaders, if they are to lead effectively, and be rightfully called by the name 'leader', must be able to use decency, delicacy, discretion, finesse, judiciousness, politeness, prudence, sensitivity, subtlety, tact, and thoughtfulness, in order to influence those that would respect them as leaders. Those who use diplomacy and all of these qualities associated with diplomacy demonstrate a refinement of spirit that elevates them to a position worthy of respect and genuine admiration.

LACK OF DIPLOMACY IS TANTAMOUNT TO BULLYING

Those that hope to be leaders, while discrediting diplomacy as political incorrectness, often turn out to be bullies, and give support to the thinking that bullying is the way to get anything done. This is wrong. True leadership involves being sensitive to the needs of those that are led.

FOLLOW GOOD EXAMPLES

As you aspire to leadership, think of good and worthy men and women, who take responsibility for getting things done, who do not shirk responsibility, but set out to ensure that those they lead have a say in how things are done. Recognize the qualities that make individuals you admire good leaders, and imitate them in your everyday life. Resist the temptation to be a bully who tries to assert his or her authority or to boss others around to make himself or herself feel important.

CHAPTER 16 - FOOD FOR THOUGHT

TOPICS AND IDEAS FOR SELF-REFLECTION AND
DISCUSSION

Self-Reflection

Do you consider yourself a leader?

What qualities do you possess that make you think of yourself as a leader?

What changes would you consider would make you a better leader?

Group Discussion

Discuss someone you consider to be an outstanding leader and describe the qualities the person possesses that make him/her a leader.

Discuss someone you consider to hold a leadership position but does not possess the qualities that make him/her a good leader.

CHAPTER 16 - REFERENCES AND FURTHER READING

Levine, M. P. & Boaks, J. (2014). What does ethics have to do with leadership? *Journal of Business Ethics, 124*(2), 225-242

Ng, E. & Kelloff, A. (2013). Fast food leadership: Valuing what is easy over what is best. *Organization Development Journal, 31*(4), 37-45

Van Quaquebeke, N. & Eckloff, T. (2010). Defining respectful leadership: what it is, how it can be measured, and another glimpse at what it is related to. *Journal of Business Ethics, 91*, 343-358.

Shockness, I. (2020). Leadership Beyond the Job: 30 Ways for Older Teens and Young Adults to develop effective leadership skills Toronto: Vanquest Publishing. Available at - https://www.amazon.com/dp/1989480012

CHAPTER 17

THINKING ABOUT GRATITUDE

How many times have we heard someone say, with deep hurt, that someone is ungrateful? Many parents would say there is nothing worse than an ungrateful child. People who have helped their siblings or friends often complain that those they have helped have not recognized or even said "Thanks" for the assistance and support they have received. Instead, those that have been helped often turn back to hurt the very ones that cared for them. Similarly, how many times have we heard someone who was helped downplay the assistance he or she received, or even spurned the person that helped him or her! These are situations that need not be, if people take time to be grateful for what they have received. These are also the situations that come to mind when we think of gratitude. However, there is more to gratitude than this.

GRATEFUL FOR GOOD HEALTH

How many times have we stopped to be grateful for the good health that we enjoy? Even if we have ailments, there is still much to be grateful for, for we could have been in a worse condition. Just being alive is something for which we should be grateful. We had no control over our birth, neither do we rightly have control over our time of death.

MUCH FOR WHICH TO BE GRATEFUL

Some of us may be fortunate enough to have all our needs supplied, and still have extras. Some of us may be making ends meet, and can still feel grateful that we are in good health. Some of us may feel grateful that we have a job and so could meet our financial commitments on a regular basis. There is much for which to be grateful!!

GRATEFUL FOR FAMILY AND FRIENDS

Others may have little or no financial resources, but may have the love of family. Or maybe we are orphaned or fostered, and are away from our biological families. We should be particularly grateful for those who have made us part of their families. They have chosen us and have decided to be there for us!! We must also be grateful for the friends that make us feel loved, despite our faults and shortcomings.

GRATEFUL FOR FEELINGS OF HOPE

All of us could feel grateful that we are able to read, write, communicate to share our ideas with each other, to have the freedom to voice our opinions, and to worship in our own faiths. We do not live in a perfect world, but we have to be grateful even when we could recognize there is something imperfect about our situation. For then, there is the hope of making changes for the better.

COMPLAINING LEADS TO FURTHER DISCONTENT

I know it is easy to complain and gain the sympathy of others for one thing or another, but complaining often leads to more discontent and more complaining. A vicious circle develops that could often lead to negativity and depression.

BE GRATEFUL FOR WISDOM

Regardless of the negative things in our lives, and we all have them, we could think of the things that we can be grateful for, and before long, be in a positive frame of mind. We can also think of the things that need to be changed, and do something positive about bringing about those changes. We must be grateful for wisdom that will make this possible. We must then take time to recognize there is someone or some force greater than we are, that provides the wisdom, and for me, that is GOD. People from different religious backgrounds also recognize that there is a greater force that is loving and caring, and for which they must be grateful.

WISDOM FOR POSITIVE CHANGE

Some people give this wisdom different names, and some even deny that this wisdom comes from God or from a source outside of themselves. However, regardless of how we think, we must all be grateful for the wisdom that helps us bring about positive changes in our lives and causes us to love each other.

BE GRATEFUL FOR THE "RAINBOWS IN OUR CLOUDS"

Just in case you are still thinking of what to be grateful for! Think of the people that were kind to you at some point in your life. Think of where you would have been today, had you not received that kindness. According to Maya Angelou, in a presentation some years ago at SkyDome, now Rogers' Centre in Toronto, we should all be grateful for the 'rainbows in our clouds', for the people who came into our lives at critical periods and helped us through our difficult times. These people are the 'rainbows' that helped us through our 'clouds'.

BE GRATEFUL BY PAYING IT FORWARD

Maybe those who have helped you are long gone. Maybe you never knew the person that may have helped you out of a difficult situation. Maybe you lament the fact that you cannot be grateful and say "Thanks" to those who actually made a difference in your life. Maybe at one time in your life, you did not recognize the importance of being grateful, and never acknowledged gratefulness.

Think about it. You can be grateful to those who have helped you in the past by being kind to others now and in the future, and your gratitude would be sincere, especially if you expect nothing in return. By carrying on the tradition of being grateful, you complete the circle of gratitude, which we hope would continue indefinitely.

CHAPTER 17 - FOOD FOR THOUGHT

TOPICS AND IDEAS FOR SELF-REFLECTION AND DISCUSSION

Self-Reflection

Do I feel gratitude for who I am and what I have?

Do I feel gratitude for the friends that I have?

Do I often complain about all the things that are wrong around me and in our society?

Do I sometimes think that I need an attitude makeover?

How can I change my attitude and become more grateful rather than more critical?

Group Discussion

How Significant Are These Statements?

"Gratitude is the healthiest of all human emotions. The more you recognize and express gratitude for the things you have, the more things you will have to express gratitude for." – Zig Ziglar

"Be thankful for what you have; you'll end up having more. If you concentrate on what you don't have, you will never, ever have enough." – Oprah Winfrey

HOW TO BE A 'FRIEND' TO PEOPLE YOU MEET

We sometimes think that the only people we should be kind to are people that we know. This means that we are often indifferent to others around us, whom we may consider as strangers. We fail to recognize that these people around us, whom we do not know, may be feeling left out or excluded. A kind word, a smile, or a 'hello' could make all the world of difference to someone who may be considered a stranger.

A TRUE STORY

A story I have heard and have retold several times is that of a teenage boy who one day saw another boy drop his books in the school locker. This first teen, who did not know the second teen, bent down and helped the second teen pick up the books that he had dropped. This was a good deed that took only a couple minutes. The first teen went about his business, not even thinking that he had done a good deed for the day.

FAST FORWARD

Several years later, the second teen, then an adult, encountered the first teen, also an adult, on the street, and greeted him as a long lost friend. The second man was taken aback by this familiarity because he did not know the first man very well. However, the second man recognized him as the teenager that he had helped pick up his books that day in the locker room at their high school. It was just a chance encounter where he did a very small good deed.

THE SECOND TEENAGER'S STORY

The second man who had dropped his books that morning as a teenager explained that he was so depressed that he had decided to commit suicide that day. He was in the process of cleaning out his locker, so that his mother would not have had the unpleasant task of doing so, after his death. It was during this process that he had dropped his books.

When the first teenager had bent down and helped him pick up his books, this made the second teenager feel that at least he had a friend. He changed his mind about suicide. It was because of this small kind deed that the first teenager had done that had saved the second teenager's life. This second teenager, now a man, was grateful for what the first teenager had done way back in high school. This was why he had considered this man his friend.

MORAL OF THIS STORY

What this story shows is that being kind to someone that we do not know could have far-reaching positive effects that we don't know about. It makes sense that we are kind, not only to the people we know, but to the people that we may encounter by chance as we go about our daily activities.

On the contrary, our callous actions, our flippant statements, our cruel jokes, can also have negative impacts and far-reaching consequences. This consideration therefore requires us to be conscious of the fact that our actions and words can be potent, even when we do not intend them to be.

CHAPTER 18 - FOOD FOR THOUGHT

TOPICS AND IDEAS FOR SELF-REFLECTION AND

DISCUSSION

Self-Reflection

What do I consider friendship? Am I a good friend? How do I show my friendship to others?

Group Discussion

"Sometimes when you see a person cry it's better not to ask "why?" Sometimes it takes only three words to make them happy again. And those three words are: "I AM HERE""- (Unknown)

"If friends disappoint you over and over, that's in large part your own fault. Once someone has shown a tendency to be self-centered, you need to recognize that and take care of yourself; people aren't going to change simply because you want them to." – Oprah Winfrey

What is the significance of these quotes?

CHAPTER 19

TAKING RESPONSIBILITY FOR YOUR STRESS:

YOUNG PEOPLE AND STRESS

Are you experiencing stress at this time of your life? You are not alone. Teenagers and young adults often experience stress, and this could sometimes be so severe that it could cause them to become depressed and unproductive.

FACTORS CONTRIBUTING TO STRESS

Some of the factors contributing to stress, particularly among teenagers, include demands at school, problems with friends or peers at school, and unsafe living conditions. Other factors include body image issues, concern over being too fat, being too thin, or not just having the right body type.

SOME PHYSICAL WAYS TO IDENTIFY STRESS

Young people can often tell when stress is becoming too much for them. Some of the symptoms include increased heart rate, faster breathing, and cold or clammy hands. Some young people become irritable and even confused, unable to think clearly.

SOME WAYS TO MANAGE STRESS

LISTENING TO MUSIC

Some young people find that listening to their favorite music helps them to relax. It allows them to forget about the things that cause them stress.

TALKING TO A FRIEND

Talking to a friend can also help, because it allows the young person to 'vent' or to express himself or herself. At times, a friend lends a sympathetic ear and can also help the young person to get a better perspective on things. Sometimes, the young person may come to see that what he or she considered as a disaster was really not nearly as bad as at first thought. In some instances, a young person only needs someone to sit there and listen, and not even say a word. Just having another person around and having the opportunity to express feelings are sometimes all a young person needs to clear his or her mind.

HAVING A SUPPORT GROUP

Some young people have a group of friends or family members they can rely on when they are facing difficult times. This is very helpful for they do not feel so alone when faced with stressful situations.

LEARNING TO ENGAGE IN POSITIVE SELF-TALK

When people are depressed, they tend to see things negatively. It is sometimes very difficult to get out of this negative place on one's own. This is why reading positive books and articles can be a means of improving one's mood. The secret is to try replacing negative self-talk with positive self-talk. People are encouraged to see the good in themselves as a means of coming out of a very negative place.

GETTING PROFESSIONAL HELP

Young people who find their depression persisting and lasting for longer periods of time, often seek out professional help. There is no shame in speaking to parents, school counsellors, doctors, religious leaders or other responsible individuals who would often guide a young person with bouts of deep depression to get appropriate help. The fact is that many people, young and old alike, experience feelings of depression from time to time, and many seek out ways of getting help.

TRY TO IDENTIFY THE SOURCE OF STRESS

However, one of the best ways to deal with stress is to try to understand the underlying source of that stress. Some people experience stress when they feel that they do not have control over their time. This is very common among students, who often feel that the demands of school and course work are just too great for them. This often results in young people experiencing self-doubt, questioning whether they have what it takes to undertake their studies. When this happens, young people should look for ways of taking control of their time. Young people are encouraged to engage in time management.

CHAPTER 19 - FOOD FOR THOUGHT

TOPICS AND IDEAS FOR SELF-REFLECTION AND DISCUSSION

Self-Reflection

What are the sources of my stress?

Am I dealing effectively with my stress?

What are some of the activities that I can do to help relieve my stress?

Group Discussion

What impact stress has on young people today? What are some of the signs?

What can your group or class do to reduce stress on members?

Design a program that young people in school could use to deal with stress.

CHAPTER 20

TAKING RESPONSIBILITY FOR YOUR TIME: TIME MANAGEMENT

TAKING RESPONSIBILITY FOR TIME MANAGEMENT

It is well recognized that the greatest source of stress for many young people is school work. While many teenagers and young adults are perfectly capable of understanding the material they are expected to master for their course, they have problems coping with the work because of what they consider time constraints.

Some young people avoid dealing with the stress and so may engage in activities that keep their mind from focusing on the problem. This could involve listening to music, getting involved in the drug culture, or engaging in activities that allow them to forget. However, this is not coping with stress, for the problem that originally contributed to the stress still remains.

ACTIVE COPING

However some young people realize that the best way for them to cope with their stress is to try to reduce it or remove it altogether.

TIME MANAGEMENT = SELF-MANAGEMENT

Time management is really about self-management. One must think of the many activities that one has to carry out. Apart from allocating adequate time for eating, sleeping and personal grooming, one must pay attention to the amount of time one must work, study and commute. In other words, the issue of time management is really about managing oneself.

HOW TO SELF-MANAGE

It is important to consider two things about self-management. The first is that one has to make good decisions about how to use one's time. The second is that one has to think about using one's time wisely and efficiently.

HOW TO BE A GOOD SELF MANAGER

One must learn not to procrastinate. It is very easy when faced with many different tasks to carry out to keep putting them off. Putting off these tasks can be seen as a way of avoiding doing them at the present time. The problem here is that these tasks still remain to be completed, and the problem becomes more serious as the number of tasks may increase.

HOW TO OVERCOME PROCRASTINATION

In order to overcome procrastination, a student needs to schedule work time. One recommendation is for college and university students to schedule a minimum of 2 to 3 hours for every lecture per week. High school students vary with the amount of homework they receive, but surveys among teachers reveal that on average high school teachers assign about 3.5 hours of homework per week. Depending on how many courses a student is taking, this could mean several hours of study time per week.

One recommendation is that high school students do not put off homework from day to day, as this could become a very serious problem at the end of the week. Overcoming procrastination involves committing oneself to doing a couple hours of study each day, if you are in school.

DO NOT OVERCOMMIT YOURSELF

Taking on tasks that are too large could overwhelm anyone. Therefore, it is recommended that young people break down their tasks into smaller parts, and undertake each part in turn. This would prevent the young person from feeling overwhelmed and therefore giving up.

PLAN TIME WISELY AND USE SMALL PORTIONS OF TIME EFFECTIVELY.

Sometimes, a task takes less time than was allocated for it. Or there may be half an hour between classes. A student may see this time as too short to do anything constructive, and may simply sit and wait for the next class. However, this is valuable time that can be used to accomplish something. Rather than sit and pass the time, a student may find that he or she can read one of the articles assigned for the week.

COMMUTING TIME ALSO VALUABLE

Taking a bus or train to school may be classified as commuting time, but it could also be seen as valuable learning or homework time. If commuting takes two hours a day, think of the amount of homework that could be accomplished during this time to and from school. Always walk with enough material that can be used during these hours. This is a good time to read material or learn vocabulary for a foreign language.

MAKING A TO-DO LIST

A commonsense approach to managing your time involves making a list of the things to do. Set up columns and under each column write the appropriate entry. You may create a daily list, but you may find that creating a weekly to-do list gives you more time and flexibility to complete your tasks. You also may not feel as rushed with a weekly to-do list. For example, as a student who works part-time, you have to cope with assignments and readings and also prepare for tests. You have to remember the hours of your part-time work, the activities that involve your household or family, as well as other personal matters (Herbold, 2000).

HOW TO MAKE UP A TO-DO LIST

To make up a weekly To-Do List, identify the important tasks that you have to undertake on a weekly basis (Herbold, 2000). Make up headings as shown below.

ASSIGNMENTS AND READINGS

TESTS

PART-TIME WORK

FAMILY COMMITMENTS

PERSONAL MATTERS

These are the five categories of tasks you may have to carry out every week, namely, assignment and readings, tests, part-time work, family commitments, and personal matters.

Under each of these headings, put down the activities that you have to do. Then based on the activities that you have written down under these headings, create a priority list. This will allow you to take a logical approach to how to carry out the various tasks you have to do.

HOW TO MAKE A PRIORITY LIST

MUST DO   SHOULD DO   NICE TO DO

Take all the tasks you have listed under your headings, e.g. Assignments and Readings, Tests, etc. and list them under the three headings above, namely, Must Do, Should Do and Nice to Do.

What this does is to help you do the tasks that are most urgent so that you do not fall behind in the many activities that you plan to do.

CHAPTER 20 - FOOD FOR THOUGHT

TOPICS AND IDEAS FOR SELF-REFLECTION AND
DISCUSSION

Self-Reflection

Do I manage my time well?

What evidence do I have that I manage my time well?

How can I improve on my time management?

Why am I always late handing in my assignments?

Group Discussion

What are some of the ways young people can improve on time management when it comes to classwork?

What time management programs are there that can be used in the classroom?

How can a group help its members with time management skills?

CHAPTER 20 - REFERENCES AND FURTHER READING

DiPipi-Hoy, C., Jitendra, A. K., & Kern, L. (2009). Effects of time management instruction on adolescents' ability to self-manage time in a vocational setting. *The Journal of Special Education, 43*(3), 145-159.

Forbus, P., Newbold, J. J., & Mehta, S. S. (2011). A study of non-traditional and traditional students in terms of their time management behaviors, stress factors, and coping strategies. *Academy of Educational Leadership Journal, suppl. Special Issues, 15*, 109-125.

Herbold, S. A. (2000). *Student Workbook to accompany Stress Management for Wellness* (by Walt Schafer), 4th edition. Florida: Harcourt Inc.

Olowookere, E. I., Alao, A. A., Odukoya, J. A., Adekeye, O. A., Agbude, G. A. (2015). Time management practices, character development, and academic performance *among university undergraduates: Covenant university experience. Creative Education, 6*(1), 79-86.

Zarbakhsh, M., Parhassani, S. A., Rahmani, M., Rad, M. M. & Poor, E. K. (2015). The relationship between time management, self-efficacy and entrepreneurship among students. *European Online Journal of Natural and Social Sciences, 4*(1), 211-218.

TAKING RESPONSIIBLITY FOR YOUR MENTAL HEALTH

One of the major factors contributing to mental health problems involves stress. As noted above, stress can have a negative impact on physical as well as on mental health. While adolescence can be a very stressful period in itself, there are times when stress could lead to serious mental health issues.

RECOGNIZING WHEN STRESS IS HAVING MENTAL HEALTH IMPACT

While worrying may appear normal under usual circumstances, if there are recurring or consistent feelings of sadness, hopelessness, and worthlessness, these could be signs that your mental health is deteriorating, and that it may be time to seek out help.

OTHER SUBTLE AND NOT-SO SUBTLE SIGNS

Some signs that mental health is being affected by stress is not so evident. Some signs can be easily missed. For example, some young people find that they are mostly angry. They may excuse this feeling of anger as a reaction against classmates, or to nagging parents who are always enquiring where they are going or why their grades are so low.

But it may be this young person's anger is a manifestation of deteriorating mental state, as he or she is in constant stress over a variety of conditions which he or she may feel unable to control.

OBVIOUS SIGNS

Other signs of increasing mental health problems could be inability to overcome long-time loss or death, deep depression, irritability, mood swings, frequent use and abuse of alcohol and other drugs, social isolation or being a loner, sleep problems, or the intense desire to hurt someone or destroy personal property. It may even be a desire to hurt oneself.

Other signs may include anxiety, great fears, lack of motivation, feelings of helplessness, sense of hopelessness and loss of interest in things that were once interesting,

If these are conditions that seem to persist for long periods of time, one may see this as time to seek counselling with a mental health professional. While some may think of this as a passing phase, it may be a more serious problem in the making. Getting professional help makes a great deal of sense, even if all that is needed is to talk out a particular situation and gain clarity on an issue that is baffling.

TAKE IMMEDIATE ACTION

If your car continues to sputter and stop at times, you won't wait for it to get better. You would take it to a mechanic, before it breaks down with you in the middle of the highway. Similarly, if you feel that all is not well with you mentally or emotionally, you may need to seek out the appropriate help before things get worse.

RECKLESS AND OUT-OF-CONTROL BEHAVIOR

Less subtle signs of declining mental state are reckless behavior. Feeling that one is out of control is also a sign that one's mental health may be at risk, and that it may be time to look for help. Or one may have taken dieting and exercising to an extreme. This may also be an indication of deteriorating mental state.

ARE YOU WAITING FOR HELP WITH YOUR MENTAL STATE

A young person may think that if all those adults in his or her life that claim to care, Mom, Dad, Nana, and Grandad, really did care as much as they say they do, then they would step in to help him or her. A young person may decide to wait for them to ask him, "What is wrong?" and "Why are you acting this way?" But this young person may have waited for a long time, and yet no one said anything. The young person may have been waiting for someone to ask, so that he could tell all the injustices that he or she believes have been done to him or her.

WAITING AND WAITING AND NO REACTION

After waiting for a long time, the young person may reason that his or her family members really don't care. No one asks any questions and the young person may think, "They really couldn't care as much as they claim. Why wouldn't they say something?"

THE TRUTH

The truth may be that the young person's family members quite likely may have observed the bizarre behavior, but they may have reasoned that the young person is going through a phase that he or she would soon get over.

Or maybe, the family members have not noticed that anything was wrong. They probably saw the young person as becoming independent, as making his or her own choices, and as needing some freedom to do so.

Parents may be at a loss as to how teenagers behave. They may not see the unusual behavior as a virtual cry for help, and may take it as a normal part of teenage behavior in the 21st century. For example, one of the emotions that some teenagers frequently display is that of moodiness, but extreme moodiness could be one of the signs that a teenager or young person is having mental health issues. A similar case could be made for aggressiveness.

Some parents may also recognize that their young person has a mental health problem, but are unwilling and reluctant to call it as such, because of the stigma that is often associated with mental illness or mental health disorders.

Either way, it may not be that the family members do not care, but that they may be thinking of giving their young person some personal space to figure things out or for things to resolve themselves. This is the time for family members and the young person to have a conversation. If family members do not take the lead, then the young person needs to speak up and get help.

CHAPTER 21 - FOOD FOR THOUGHT

TOPICS AND IDEAS FOR SELF-REFLECTION AND
DISCUSSION

Self-Reflection

How can I protect my mental health? What measures do I take to reduce stress and other emotions that could compromise my mental health?

Group Discussion

What is the difference between mental health and wellness?

What support groups are there in our area to help young people deal with mental health issues?

What online services exist where young people can call and access help?

What community services can families call when their family members with mental health problems are in crisis and need help?

CHAPTER 22

TAKING RESPONSIBILITY TO GET HELP FOR YOUR MENTAL HEALTH

YOUNG PERSON'S RESPONSIBILITY TO START THE CONVERSATION

In fact, some parents may feel awkward starting a conversation about their young person's mental health, even if they suspect that the young person is under considerable stress. Also, many parents may be in denial even when there are obvious signs that their young person is having mental health issues.

SPEAK UP

It remains for the young person to take the first step. The advice to a young person could be to have a conversation with her parents. Let them know how she feels. She should try to put her feelings into words. Or simply tell her parents that she needs to speak to a mental health professional. Or maybe the young person may just know that he is feeling 'weird' or feels like doing crazy things. This would be enough to indicate to his parents that their son needs help urgently.

Some young people may choose to communicate their feelings on Facebook, and while this may seem as the young person's feeling of freedom to express what he or she may be experiencing, sometimes these posts could be a cry for help. Those who communicate with these young people on Facebook should see this as a cry for help, especially when that young person threatens harms to others or to the society. Do the right thing and alert others who can help and who can stop the intended harm. You need not feel that you are betraying someone who threatens harm. You may be the last link that young person has with mental health care, and this may be what he or she is looking for but does know where to find it. A young person in a very hopeless stage may not even have the strength to look for help. However, if help were to come along, he or she may welcome it.

AFRAID OF SPEAKING TO PARENTS?

At times, children and young people may find it difficult to speak to their parents about certain subjects. Depending on the relationship young people have with their parents, sex is the usual taboo subject. However, mental health may be a close second.

PERSONAL EXPERIENCE

Some years ago, I was working with a teenage student who was having much difficulty in her Grade 12 Math. I knew she had been a good and conscientious student for several years earlier, because I had taught her.

One day I saw her struggling so hard that I simply asked her why she was having such difficulty concentrating on the work at hand. She readily began to talk to me, and I realized she had wanted to say something for some time, but felt uncomfortable starting a conversation. When she started to cry, I realized that something was seriously wrong. After a lengthy conversation, I asked her why she did not speak to her parents.

HER RESPONSE

She felt that her parents would not understand that she was really overwhelmed with school, her personal life and more. She explained that they were "expecting so much better from me". Her parents had mentioned at times that they wanted her to be a lawyer as her father, and she was not interesting in this field. She also felt that she could not do it.

She said she just couldn't bring herself to telling her parents how she was feeling at the time. She had told them on one occasion, but they simply told her that she was not applying herself to her school work and that was why she felt she did not want to follow that profession. On previous occasions, she had hinted to them about some of the things she was interested in following as a career, but as she said, they didn't give her ideas any thought, but repeated what they had told her before: she had to apply herself in order to become a lawyer. At this point, she asked me if I could speak to her parents for her. I promised to open the conversation with her parents and she agreed to that.

I did, and her parents wanted to know why she did not come to them earlier. She explained that she did. Her parents realized then that they had not taken her seriously. But they promised to listen to her, to get her help, if she needed, and to support her choice of career. She also explained to them how very angry she was at them and that sometimes she felt like leaving home.

IF YOU FEEL OUT OF CONTROL, ASK FOR HELP

If you feel uncomfortable, shy, awkward or fearful speaking to your parents about feeling out of control or overwhelmed, by all means ask someone to accompany you to start a conversation with your parents. However, most parents would readily listen to you and get you help if they believe that you are in need of such help. Don't be afraid to open up to them and tell them exactly how you feel.

YOUR RESPONSIBILITY TO PROTECT YOUR MENTAL HEALTH

You are the person who knows how you really feel. You know some of the things that may be causing you stress. You may just know how you are feeling, but have not been able to understand why you are feeling this way.

INSIST ON A PROFESSIONAL

This is the time to speak to a professional. If you are on your own, and if your feel overwhelmed or out of control, seek out help. Simply going to your doctor, any doctor, or mental health professional can be helpful. Telling that person how you really feel could very likely lead to your receiving the care that you need, or a referral to someone who could help. There is no reason to suffer in silence.

Mental health is a gift that we cannot afford to squander. When it is at risk, we must seek appropriate care.

IMPORTANCE OF MAINTAINING GOOD MENTAL HEALTH

The brain is a unique organ that undergoes development at different stages. While the period of ages 0 to 2 years is considered an important part of development, in similar fashion, the adolescent brain undergoes critical development that is necessary for adult functioning. The adolescent brain is also said to be sensitive to cortisol, the stress hormone that could wreak havoc on the brain during this critical period of development. Protecting mental health in adolescence is important for good mental health in adulthood.

CHAPTER 22 - FOOD FOR THOUGHT

TOPICS AND IDEAS FOR SELF-REFLECTION AND DISCUSSION

Self-Reflection

"Mental health is a gift that we cannot afford to squander. When it is at risk, we must seek appropriate care" (From Chapter 22).

Do I agree with this statement?

Where would I find appropriate care, if I felt at risk?

Group Discussion

What measures can we take as a group to help those who have mental health issues? What if you noticed a friend was probably having a mental health crisis, what would you do?

How can a group proceed to get mental health care for a vulnerable group or individual in the community?

CHAPTER 22 - REFERENCES AND FURTHER READING

Frosch, E., dosReis, S., & Maloney, K. (2011).Connections to outpatient mental health care of youths with repeat emergency department visits for psychiatric crises. *Psychiatric Services, 62*(6), 646-649

Gilmer, T. P., Ojeda, V. D., Leach, J. Heller, R., Garcia, P. et al. (2012). Assessing needs for mental health & other services among transition-age youths, parents and providers. *Psychiatric Services, 63*(4), 338--342

Markowitz, F. E. (2015). Involvement in mental health self-help groups and recovery. *Health Sociology Review, 24*(2), 199-212

Williams, K. A. & Chapman, M. V. (2011). Comparing health and mental health needs, service use, and barriers to services among sexual minority youths and their peers. *Health & Social Work, 36*(3), 197-206.

Yip. K., Lee, L. & Law, S. O. (2004). Self help groups in Hong Kong. *Administration and Policy in Mental Health, 31*(4), 351-360

CHAPTER 23

HOW TO COPE WITH MENTAL HEALTH STIGMA

POOR MENTAL HEALTH IS NOTHING TO BE ASHAMED OF

Many people experience poor mental health, sometimes as a result of genetics or injury, but also because of stress. Stress is seen as a major factor causing people to feel unable to cope with their daily living conditions. Relieving stress and learning to cope with it are ways that some people are able to maintain good mental health. Even some people who are susceptible to mental illness because of genetics or injury are able to prevent or control their mental illness or disorders by controlling the level of stress in their lives. Many individuals who have been diagnosed with mental disorders are able to live normal lives by taking the medications that have been prescribed for them. Being compliant with their medications is an important factor in controlling many mental disorders.

TAKE YOUR MEDS

It is when individuals who are diagnosed with mental disorders decide that they no longer need their medications that they could experience serious relapses and do terrible things. Once some individuals resume their medications, they find that the urges that cause them to behave violently may disappear.

THE STIGMA ASSOCIATED WITH MENTAL ILLNESS

The stigma that is associated with mental illness is not new. Stigma is a negative stereotype that is considered a sign of disgrace, which causes some people to be excluded from others. In previous times, when there was poor understanding of many mental disorders, people thought of the mentally ill as people that were possessed by the devil. They were ostracized from society. In the 21st century, there is much knowledge about mental disorders and also about many cures as well as the means of controlling these disorders. Mental illness is no longer a mystery, but a well understood set of conditions, most of which can be controlled through medication. Yet, there is still stigma associated with mental illness, which causes many who have been diagnosed with a mental health disorder to hide their condition for fear of being stigmatized.

STIGMA IS UNWARRANTED

Provided that those with mental disorders take their medications and follow treatment protocol, they can go on functioning normally in society indefinitely. But the stigma of mental illness causes many people to hide their condition and to even refuse to be diagnosed when they know something is very seriously wrong with them. Research has shown that about 60% of people with mental illness would not seek help because they are afraid of being labelled as mentally ill. This is a serious problem for it means that this 60% of people who are mentally ill are going around without the help they desperately need.

IT IS IGNORANT TO DISCRIMINATE AGAINST ANYONE WITH A MENTAL DISORDER

It is only ignorant people that would discriminate against someone who suffers from a mental disorder. What this shows is that those who discriminate lack the knowledge about the disorders. They are unaware of the fact that there are medications that can control many of these conditions.

THOSE WITH MENTAL DISORDERS NEED NOT HIDE

Although there are some who stigmatize mental illness, this is no reason to hide one's mental illness or disorder. It is in hiding these conditions that the worse could result. As mentioned above, many people with mental illness continue to hide their conditions because they are afraid of being diagnosed and of being stigmatized. People who have been stigmatized because of mental disorders contend that the stigmatization is far worse than living with the condition. Speaking about their conditions may turn out to be the best thing persons with mental disorders could do, since they could receive the help they so badly need to live a normal life.

If more people with mental disorders who are compliant with their medications speak up about their conditions, they would help to eliminate the fear that many others feel about mental illness, about those with mental disorders, and about being identified as mentally ill.

IMPACT OF STIGMA ON MENTALLY ILL PEOPLE

While people with mental illness could often control their symptoms through medication, many cannot overcome the mental anguish that they suffer over a life time because of being stigmatized. One of the myths perpetrated against mentally ill people is that they are dangerous and violent, and according to the Canadian Mental Health Association, mentally ill people are more likely to be the recipient of violent behavior than they are likely to be the ones displaying violent behavior. Another myth is that the poor and unintelligent are more likely to be mentally ill. People who are mentally ill are thought to be all belonging to the same group, whereas this is not the case, as there are many different disorders with different degrees of severity. People still use epithets such as "nuts" and "cracked," and it is not unusual to find these epithets are often used in the media.

WHERE STIGMATIZATION IS COMMON

As mentioned, from time to time an article may appear where mentally ill people are discriminated against. When governments closed many mental institutions and mainstreamed those who were mentally ill into special residences to accommodate them, many people opposed the accommodation. It was a case of NIMBYism all over again, as people in many neighborhoods opposed this kind of housing in their areas. Their cry was "Not in My Back Yard".

IN THE WORKPLACE

But stigma is also seen in the workplace, as people who may have been hospitalized for some mental disorder may find that on recovering they have lost their jobs. Statistics also show that 80 to 90 per cent of people with schizophrenia are unemployed, despite the fact that this mental disorder can be controlled with medication. But one of the claims that could be made is that the very fact that mental health is not receiving the attention it deserves in North America and elsewhere may be seen as an indication that it is overlooked as of high priority. Many young people experience severe mental health problems, and some parents are finding it very difficult to get the help they need for their children, even when these are quite young.

WHAT IS URGENTLY NEEDED?

What is urgently needed is more attention to mental health issues. More mental health services should be made available and there should be easy access to these services. More people need to seek out mental health care, but what stands in the way of them seeking out such care is stigma. Fear of stigma prevents many parents and their children from getting the diagnosis that will provide mental health care.

Parents can be a major support for their children with mental illness. In fact, parents may be the first to observe that their children have a mental problem, and they are the ones that can take measures to find their children help. While some parents find help for their children with a mental disorder, other parents are often in denial that their children can have a mental disorder. The result is often that some young people grow up with a mental health disorder, with their parents either trying to hide it, not recognizing it for what it is, or in denial that it exists. Some young people who are aware that something is wrong may feel embarrassed revealing that they have a problem, may also be afraid of stigma and so deny their problem.

SPEAK UP ABOUT POSSIBLE MENTAL HEALTH CHALLENGE

Most young people can recognize when something is wrong with them. While there is stigma associated with mental illness in our society, not living the best possible life they could live is something that ought to be considered. Receiving the care that could improve functioning is something that could make a major difference in the quality of life. Young people must take a stand and demand the mental health services that they need, for this is the least they can do for a good life. They can also help to reduce the stigma of mental illness by standing up and speaking up about their conditions. When young people take a positive approach to seeking out good mental health services, then attitudes would have to change and stigma would be reduced.

How to Reduce Stigma Against People with Mental Health Problems

Media Have a Role

Our media are responsible for bringing issues to the attention of the public. If the media would make mental health services a major focus of their reporting, follow up with different aspects of the problem, and not drop it when another hot topic comes around, then maybe it would become an enduring national conversation that would bring about change.

The Entertainment Industry Has a Role

Together with the media, the entertainment industry plays a role in how it presents mental illness. The depiction of people with mental illness in the media as well as in the entertainment industry is a negative one, for people with mental issues are often portrayed as dangerous, violent and unpredictable. These are the stereotypical images that shape public opinion and that cause ordinary people to hold on to these stigmatized views of people with mental illness.

However, in recent weeks, celebrities from the movies, sports and elsewhere, are speaking up about their struggles with mental health disorders and about ways with which they are dealing with their conditions. It is hoped that more celebrities coming forward and owning their mental disabilities would help with reducing stigma associated with mental health issues.

POLITICIANS HAVE A ROLE

Politicians must be made to recognize that they have a role to play in passing legislation. Despite the talk on the part of some politicians that government should be small and not be active in the personal lives of people, many politicians seem to forget that government has a legislative role, and that they, the politicians, have a responsibility to put in place the institutions that would promote the good life for the population. Legislation and regulation are needed to maintain effective institutions that would provide greater mental health services for all.

YOUNG PEOPLE, SPEAK WITH YOUR VOTE

Young people have the power to make changes in our society. A look at the situation with mental health reveals that in many cases when the words 'mental health' is used, it is in reference to a young person who was said to carry out a deadly act, because of gun violence. The majority of people that are being negatively affected are young people. The majority of people who are said to be committing serious acts because of mental health issue are also young people. Those that are seen as victims are young people. It is time young people demand that more facilities be made available for them and those of their peers that have mental health issues.

It is true that much of the violence that is being carried out by those that are said to have mental health issues is being done with guns, which have led to the call for more sensible gun laws. Such a call does not seem as rocket science. Yet, what needs to be stressed is that even as more regulation should be sought with respect to access to guns, there is a need for more support for mental health services.

As a young person, think about the situation, and vote guided by your good sense. Choose your leaders who would look after your interest: your mental health and your safety.

CHAPTER 23 - FOOD FOR THOUGHT

TOPICS AND IDEAS FOR SELF-REFLECTION AND
DISCUSSION

Self-Reflection

Have I ever stigmatized someone who had a mental health episode without realizing it at the time?

What are some situations that I now recognize that I stigmatized someone with a mental health problem?

If I had similar situations, how would I act differently?

Group Discussion

Discuss some of the many ways that people with mental health issues ae stigmatized, and what measures can be taken and by whom to eliminate stigmatization?

Some of the areas to think about this are in healthcare, in a job situation,

What impact does stigmatization of the mentally ill have on these individuals?

CHAPTER 23 - REFERENCES AND FURTHER READING

Canadian Mental Health Association (n.d.). The stigma associated with mental illness. *https://ontario.cmha.ca/mental-health/mental-health-conditions/stigma-and-discrimination/*

Clark, W., Welch, S.N., Berry, S.H., Collentine, A.M., & Collins, R. (2013). California's historic effort to reduce the stigma of mental illness: The Mental Health Services Act. *American Journal of Public Health, 103*(5), 786-794.

Corrigan, P.W., Druss, B.G. & Perlick, D.A. (2014). The impact of mental illness stigma on seeking and participating in mental health care. Retrieved from *http://www.psychologicalscience.org/index.php/publications/mental-illness-stigma.html*

Henderson, C., Evans-Lacko, S. & Thornicroft, G. (2013). Mental illness stigma, help seeking, and public health programs. *American Journal of Public Health, 103*(5), 777-780/

Theurer, J.M., Jean-Paul, N., Cheyney, K., Koro-Ljungberg, M., Stevens, B.R. (2015). Wearingthe label of mental illness: Community-based participatory action research of mental illness Stigma. *The Qualitative Report, 20*(1), 42-58

HOW TO PROMOTE YOUR MENTAL WELLNESS

Mental wellness, mental health, and mental health wellness, are often used synonymously, but are sometimes thought of differently. Mental health is the most commonly used of these three terms, and has taken on some negative connotation, as 'mental health' is often used to define 'some state of mental illness'. Mental illness refers to the breakdown in a person's mental health to some degree, and so, in common discourse, when reference is made to a person's mental health, the implication is that this person has a deficit in mental health functioning. In other words, mental health in this context is used to define a continuum of mental illness, ranging from being mildly to being severely mentally ill.

WHAT IS MENTAL WELLNESS?

Mental wellness is used to define the state of being well mentally. In this respect, mental wellness is used to describe good and positive mental health, and is similar to the concept of a person being in good physical health.

It is in this context that the World Health Organization (WHO), using the term 'mental health' as 'mental wellness" defines mental health as "a state of well-being in which the individual realizes his or her own abilities, can cope with the normal stresses of life, can work productively and fruitfully, and is able to make a contribution to his or her community."

Mental wellness is seen as maintaining a healthy balance among our thoughts, our behaviors, and our reactions, or a balance in our emotional, psychological and social well-being. Mental wellness is therefore based on how we think, feel and act or behave. As Swarbrick (2006) observes, "Wellness is holistic and multi-dimensional, and includes physical, emotional, intellectual, social, environmental, and spiritual dimensions" (p. 31).

WHAT IS MENTAL HEALTH WELLNESS?

The term 'mental health wellness' is probably used to depart from the negative connotation often associated with mental health, and to signify that this use of the term 'mental health' should not be thought of as associated with the incidence of mental illness.

ASPECTS OF MENTAL WELLNESS

In looking at the interaction among the different aspects of mental wellness, we will see that the relationship we have with others, particularly our loved ones, our work and social environment, as well as our coping skills, all come together to determine how mentally well we are.

Our coping skills will determine how well we deal with stress and the emotions that we display, for example, anger, irritability, anxiety and/or depression, when we are under stress.

Stress takes a toll on us physically, and can be manifested in terms of headaches, neck pains, palpitations of the heart, and stomach problems, all of which can contribute to overall poor physical well-being. It is for this reason that many individuals with poor mental health also experience chronic stress and poor physical well-being.

Mental wellness is therefore based on having good relationships, particularly with our loved ones, having a positive work and social environment, and having good coping skills that help us to deal effectively with challenges that we face on a daily basis without feeling overwhelmed.

MENTAL WELLNESS IN A STRESSFUL ENVIRONMENT

Many people see poor mental health as something that afflicts others, but we are all highly susceptible to having poor mental health, except we take precautions to protect ourselves. This is similar to the situation with physical health. We are all highly susceptible to developing diseases and having poor physical health, except we take precautions to protect ourselves. It is estimated that our society has about 20 per cent of the population as mentally ill, or 1 in every 5 people having some form of mental illness.

It is for this reason that we should place high priority on developing and maintaining mental wellness in our highly stressful social environment.

WAYS TO MAINTAIN MENTAL WELLNESS

- Maintain a positive attitude
- Make healthy lifestyle choices
- Talk to trained professionals about feelings that trouble you
- Establish a good support system of family and friends, especially during challenging times
- Reach out to others, knowing that you are not alone.
- If you feel overwhelmed and don't know what to do, call a crisis line and/or seek out professional help.

WHY TAKING A WELLNESS APPROACH HELPS

People who have experienced poor mental health or mental illness and who recover see the wellness approach as focusing on health and wellness, rather than focusing on the illness.

The advantage in taking a wellness approach is that it helps the individual to assume the social roles that he or she at one time valued. The individual is then motivated to seek again the goals, preferences, interests and strengths that he or she once had, rather than trying to overcome a disease.

By focusing on overall wellness, which includes physical health, emotional maturity, spirituality, living and working environment, intellectual capacity and social supports, the individual tries to be whole again.

THE MENTAL WELLNESS APPROACH CAN
WORK FOR EVERYONE

By maintaining a positive outlook on life, by seeing the glass as half-full rather than as half- empty, by being optimistic rather than being pessimistic, by feeling hopeful rather than helpless, by controlling our thoughts and managing our behavior, individuals can balance their emotional, psychological and social well-being.

Reading positive books is one way of developing a positive mental attitude and feeling that they can control their lives. Individuals have the responsibility for taking control of their lives and maintaining a wellness approach in all that they think, feel and do. When individuals feel they need some help, they should get that help. A person's mental health is precious, delicate, and should be protected at all times.

SPECIFIC METHODS TO DEVELOP A WELLNESS LIFESTYLE

A prominent method of developing a wellness lifestyle is developing good habits, for good habits contribute to health and wellness. Factors that influence habit formation are motivation, willpower, and rewards. According to Nemec, Swarbrick and Merlo (2015), in order to foster the formation of good habits, we must analyze our current behaviors, examine short term goals or objectives that are specific and measurable, and develop a detailed action plan.

Developing a wellness lifestyle will not come from merely wishing it, but it will come from deliberate action taken to achieve this goal. As Swarbrick (2015) maintains, wellness is "a conscious, deliberate process that requires a person to become aware of and make choices for a more satisfying lifestyle" (p. 13).

Therefore, we should place great emphasis on mental wellness as an appropriate approach to maintaining good mental health.

CHAPTER 24 - FOOD FOR THOUGHT

TOPICS AND IDEAS FOR SELF-REFLECTION AND

DISCUSSION

Self-Reflection

If I thought I had mental health problem, would I hide it from my family and friends? Why or why not?

Would my family be supportive or would they be embarrassed because of this? Would they try to hide it from their friends?

Would my friends be supportive or would they be embarrassed and stay away from me?

How would I feel telling my family and friends that I have a mental health problem, if this were the case?

Group Discussion

What is the difference between mental health and mental wellness? What are some ways of promoting mental wellness?

How can we change the perception of family, friends, and even group members about people with mental health problems, if they have negative views about people with any of these conditions that qualify as mental health issues?

CHAPTER 24 - REFERENCES AND FURTHER READING

Canadian Mental Health Association of British Columbia (2009). Mental Health Wellness Week – Strategies for good mental health wellness. Retrieved from *http://www.mhww.org/strategies.html*

Jurewicz, I. (2015). Mental health in young adults and adolescents – supporting general physicians to provide holistic care. *Clinical Medicine, 15*(2), 151 - 154 *https://lethbridge.cmha.ca/mental_health/mental-wellness-tips/*

Nemec, P. B., Swarbrick, M. A. & Merlo, D. M. (2015). The force of habit: Creating and sustaining a wellness lifestyle. *Journal of Psychosocial Nursing & Mental Health Services, 53*(9), 24-30.

Swarbrick, M. (2015). *Wellness coaching manual.* Freehold, New Jersey: Collaborative Support Programs of New Jersey, Institute for Wellness & Recovery Initiatives.

Swarbrick, M. (2006). A wellness approach. *Psychiatric Rehabilitation Journal, 29*(4), 311-314.

CHAPTER 25

TAKING RESPONSIBILITY FOR YOUR PERSONAL SAFETY

Do you pay attention to your personal safety? Or do you take it for granted that you are young and invincible?

PERSONAL SAFETY NOT TO BE TAKEN FOR GRANTED

Personal safety is something that we often take for granted, reasoning that we are not children, and old enough to be in control of our bodies. Unfortunately, many of us do not pay attention to our safety, much to our detriment. Many of the rules for personal safety are commonsense rules, but we overlook them because they seem so obvious.

"I'M GROWN – I AM MY OWN BOSS"

Many adults think of themselves as their own bosses who need not give account to anyone about their whereabouts. Many young people see this behavior as evidence of coming of age, and fret when parents ask them where they are going. In fact, many young people are simply mirroring the behavior of their parents or other significant adults. While to adults and particularly to young people, not having to give account of where they are going may seem a sign of independence, there are times when it is important to say where you are going.

TELL OTHERS WHERE YOU ARE GOING

Therefore, the first rule of personal safety, whether you are an adult or a young person, is to tell others where you are going and when you are expected home, especially if you will be making an unusual trip or undertaking an unusual task. For one thing, if you do not return home on time, it signals that something may be wrong, and others may be able to provide assistance. For another, telling others where you are going when you leave home is simple courtesy.

CALL HOME WHEN YOU WILL BE LATE

This brings us to rule number two. If you are out and you are going to be late, whether adult or young person, you should call home, and inform others of your lateness. This practice could ease many troubled minds, especially for parents whose children are out.

ALWAYS BE AWARE OF YOUR SURROUNDINGS

The third personal safety rule to bear in mind is to be always aware of your surroundings. If you feel that there is someone suspicious in your immediate environment, take action to extricate yourself from the situation. If you feel that you are being followed, go to the closest occupied building and call police. If you are not sure that the person you see walking behind you is really following you, cross the street and change direction. If the other person does the same thing, then you are relatively sure that you are being followed. Go to the nearest store and call police.

With most young people and even children having their own cell phones today, you may be able to call police while you are being followed. However, if taking time to use the cell phone would slow you down and allow the person following you to catch up to you, you may find getting to a crowded place as soon as possible and calling from there may be a better option. Use your discretion to decide on the safer course of action.

It does not matter that you are an older teenager or young adult, following safety rules is important.

DON'T FIGHT OVER THINGS

The fourth personal safety rule is for young women who carry purses, or young people who carry iPods, expensive phones and other electronic devices. It is important to carry your purse close to you, but never attach it to your wrist or neck. For young people carrying iPods and other devices, keep them out of sight. If someone is going to rob you, let them have what they are after. Don't fight over things. Your life is worth much more.

HAVE A BUDDY WHENEVER POSSIBLE

A fifth personal safety rule is not to go walking or jogging alone, if you can help it. Have a buddy. However, if you have to go out by yourself, walk or run in well-lit areas, and avoid alleys, parks and bushes. Do not take shortcuts through parks, vacant lots, or deserted places, and stay in areas that are frequented by other people. This is simple common sense.

Do Not Hitchhike

A very popular piece of advice that so many young people overlook is personal safety rule number six: do not hitchhike or take rides from strangers, regardless of how pleasant or harmless they may appear. Even when someone may introduce himself or herself as knowing one of your friends, still use caution because you do not know that person. Be polite, but do not take a ride. There are times, though, when you simply have to be abrupt and get yourself out of harm's way.

Keep Your Distance

The seventh personal safety rule concerns drivers who stop for direction. It is very common to get lost and to ask someone for directions. Most of us who drive have encountered this from time to time. However, if a driver stops for directions, you may render assistance, but do not go too close to the car, because you can be pulled inside.

Be Prepared

When you are going home, you should have your key out and be ready to push it into the keyhole without delay. Also, remember, when you are going out at night, leave a light on, so on your return, it would be easier to see the keyhole. This is safety rule number eight.

STAY CLOSE TO OTHER PEOPLE WHEN ON PUBLIC TRANSPORT

The next safety rule pertains to when you are travelling on public transit at night. Sit close to the bus driver, if possible. If you are on the subway, wait in the designated waiting areas on the platform, if these are available, because these areas are monitored by video and are considered safer. Pay attention to where the telephone is on the platform, or carry a cell phone. Use the alarm in the subway or on the bus if you are threatened or have some emergency. Caution: misuse of this alarm carries a penalty. Depending on where you live, you may not have these facilities. Then, you should stay close to other people on public transportation.

CHECK YOUR CAR BEFORE ENTERING

When you travel by car, remember personal safety rule number ten. Lock your car doors when you leave, even if you are going to be away for a short period. Before re-entering your car, look inside. If there is someone hiding inside your car, you would be able to see that person and get help. It is best, if you notice someone inside your car when you return, to leave the car as if you had not noticed the intruder. Pretend that you forgot to get something, and call police. The chance is, police may be able to apprehend this intruder, and prevent him or her from preying on someone else.

PAY ATTENTION

Although we may live in a fairly safe neighborhood, it makes good sense to pay attention to personal safety. The personal safety rules mentioned above are just a few of the ones that we should use regularly. Good sense would dictate other precautions that we should be taking. If we know our neighborhood may not be safe and that it has challenges, we need to take extra precaution and not expose ourselves to danger. Don't walk late at night. Don't take shortcuts through parks, especially when it is dusk or dark. In other words, do not present ourselves as potential victims.

CHAPTER 25 - FOOD FOR THOUGHT

TOPICS AND IDEAS FOR SELF-REFLECTION AND DISCUSSION

Self-Reflection

After reading through this chapter, can I say that I use the measures mentioned to show responsibility for my safety? Do I resent telling my family members where I am going when I leave the house?

Am I generally concerned about my safety and do I take reasonable measures?

Group Discussion

What measures should people, young and old, take to promote their safety? Discuss different situations, for example, safety at work, safety on the streets, safety in driving and boating, etc.

YOUNG WORKER, BE SAFE

If you are a young person heading off to your first job, or if you are presently a part-time or even a full-time employee, there are some alarming statistics to which you need to give your utmost consideration. Far too many bright young people get hurt or killed on their part-time jobs. While many young people are enthusiastic about their work and want to show how capable they are, many become distracted, do not foresee danger, or may not be adequately trained. The result is that they expose themselves unnecessarily to danger. Don't be one of the statistics.

DID YOU KNOW?

- Every 7 minutes an American teenager is injured on the job to the extent that he or she has to be taken to the emergency department.

- In 2009, 359 workers under the age of 24 died as a result of work related injuries, with 27 of these being young workers under the age of 18.

- Young workers under the age of 25 are twice as likely to be injured as workers 25 and older.

- Over 1.5 million teenagers work in the United States, with 44% of teens between the ages of 15 and 17 working in the retail trade and food services.

- The majority of young workers that are injured on the job in America are injured in the retail food industry.

- Don't become a statistic!

THINGS TO KNOW TO KEEP SAFE

- Know the rules and regulations related to your job, and follow them. This is important not only to protect you, but also to protect your co-workers.

- If you see anything that looks unsafe, it is your responsibility to tell your employer or supervisor about it.

- If you are required to wear protective equipment, don't see it as a bother, but as something that may save your life. Wear the equipment that you are required to wear. This could involve hairnets, gloves, aprons, safety glasses, ear plugs and the like.

- If you have an accident, it is necessary to report it to your employer or supervisor immediately, and if necessary get medical advice on this.

- Be aware of hazards and take precaution.

- Get the necessary training. Don't take the attitude that you already know how to do the work.

- Don't assume that because you have seen something done that you can do it. Make sure you can actually do it yourself.

- If you don't know something or if you are unsure, ask questions. Don't be afraid of asking "dumb questions".

- Get the supervision that you need. If the supervisor will be away, find out who would provide assistance, if you need it.

- Do the job for which you were hired. Don't try to impress others that you can do more than you were hired to do.

- Talk to your family. Let them know what you are doing. Tell them if you think something is not right.
- Be honest. If the work is too hard or complicated for you, let your supervisor know. Don't try to do the work, when you know in your heart that it is too much for you.

Know these rules and stay safe!

Questions to Consider to Stay Safe

- Will I have to work late or early in the morning?
- Will I have to work alone?
- What safety equipment will I have to wear?
- Will there be noise?
- What chemicals will I have to work with?
- Will I get training on this job?
- Is there a fire extinguisher around?

WHEN ACCEPTING EMPLOYMENT, ASK THESE POTENTIALLY LIFE-SAVING QUESTIONS!

SPECIAL FACTORS TO CONSIDER TO STAY SAFE

WATCH FOR HOT OIL AND HEAVY EQUIPMENT

If you work in a fast food restaurant, where you work with hot oil, wait until the oil is cooled before lifting it out. Get help moving heavy equipment and objects. Use appropriate protective gloves and other gear when moving heavy equipment.

CONVEYOR BELTS AND EQUIPMENT WITH MOVING PARTS

If you are working with a conveyor belt or a machine with moving parts, make sure you do not have loose clothing that could get caught up in the machine. When working with machines, also keep your hair wrapped up or covered. Many young workers have had the experience of their hair being caught in the machines with which they were working. Where there are sharp cutting parts, be aware of your hands and the possibility of injury.

WORKING WITH MACHINES

Always ask for training on a machine, even if you have some idea as to how the machine works, or how to use it. In many cases, machines may differ from manufacturer to manufacturer. Be sure about the machine and the safety features related to the specific machine. Never operate any machine without a safeguard in place. If you are to clean a machine, make sure there is no way that the machine can move or be turned on. In other words, whenever you use or clean a machine, be sure that you are in total control of that machine, and that someone else cannot inadvertently do something that could put the machine in operation while you are working on it.

Accidents have occurred where a worker has turned off a machine to clean it, and while cleaning it, another worker, unaware that the first worker was cleaning the machine, turned it on. The first worker was killed. Don't become a statistic.

PREVENT FALLS

Be careful when operating a ladder. If it is a sliding ladder, make sure it is locked in place before you climb it. Also, watch your fingers as you slide the ladder up or down. If you don't know how to operate the ladder, or how to put it away, ask for help.

KNOW YOUR RIGHTS ON THE JOB

- You have a right to know
- You have a right to participate
- You have a right to refuse unsafe work.

KNOW YOUR RESPONSIBILITIES

- You should know about job safety.
- You should know about hazards that threaten your safety and that of your co-workers.
- You should find ways to make your job even safer.
- You should know how to deal with emergencies, and what to do in different situations

WORK ATTITUDES

WORK SMART TO AVOID ACCIDENTS

You must work smart to avoid accidents. Firstly, as a young worker, you need to ask questions. You should speak to your boss, when you need more training to do the job that is expected of you, when you would like someone to observe you and make sure you are doing the job right, when you know there is a hazard in the work you are doing, or when you suspect there is something or some situation that could put you or another worker at risk of injury. If you have an idea that would make your workplace safer, you also need to speak up.

MAINTAINING RESPECTFUL RELATIONSHIPS

A relationship with your boss is very different from your relationship with other people in your life. You should be polite, respectful, not taking a confrontational stance in words or behavior, and try not to put your supervisor or boss on the spot. When requesting a discussion on a personal issue, ask to speak to your boss or supervisor privately, and not in front of all your other coworkers. Always end your meeting with your boss on a positive note. Let your supervisor know that you are serious about being a good and trusted worker, but that the conditions that you find unsafe should be addressed. Don't be a smart aleck and try to embarrass your boss or supervisor.

ASK ABOUT JOB SAFETY ON INTERVIEW

When you are being interviewed for a job, if the issue does not come up, you should ask pertinent questions about job safety. You should ask specifically whether job safety training would be provided, when you would receive that training if you were hired, whether you'd be working with chemicals, whether you would receive specific hazardous material training, whether you have to wear safety gear, whether your employer would provide this equipment, and whether there would be orientation about emergency procedures. Before you start work, or even after you have gotten the job and are actually working, you should also make sure that you are aware of safety procedures and take measures to ensure you and other workers are safe.

For example, if you are expected to operate a forklift or run heavy equipment, you must ensure that you receive the proper training. Although the pay for this job may be quite exciting and enticing, don't say you know how to operate equipment if you don't know how to do so well. Even if you have used this kind of equipment, or a similar one, in the past, be wise and obtain the required training that the company provides.

CHAPTER 26 - FOOD FOR THOUGHT

TOPICS AND IDEAS FOR SELF-REFLECTION AND DISCUSSION

Self-Reflection

As a young worker, do I know all there is to keeping safe at my workplace?

Should I enquire about safety at work, if my workplace does not bring up the subject?

If I notice an unsafe situation at work, should I point this out to the supervisor? Could I lose my job because of this? Would I do about them? Is there more training that I should seek out?

Group Discussion

Discuss the challenges young workers face in the workplace and how their safety is compromised.

What measures can young workers take to stay safe?

What are some legal protections for young people on the job?

CHAPTER 26 - REFERENCES AND FURTHER READING

Center for Disease Control & Prevention, National Institute for Occupational Safety & Health, Labor Occupational Health Program, University of California, Berkeley, Education (2010). Joint Publication. Talking Safety: Teaching Young workers about safety and Health. Retrieved from *http://www.cdc.gov/niosh/talkingsafety/states/nj /entireNJ.pdf*

Einberg, E., Lidell. E. & Clausson. E. K. (2015). Awareness of demands and unfairness and the importance of connectedness and security: Teenage girls' lived experiences of their everyday lives. *International Journal of Qualitative Studies on Health and Well-being, 10,* 1 – 12.

IAPA Programs (2008-2010). Young workers (injured on the job). Retrieved from *http://www.iapa.ca/main/outreach_yw/ywworke r.aspx*

Krogstad, R. E., Monness, E. & Sorensen, T. (2013). Social networks for mental health clients: Resources and solutions. *Community Mental Health Journal, 49*(1), 95-100.

LaRue, D. E., & Herrman, J. W. (2008). Adolescent stress through the eyes of high-risk teens. *Continuing Nursing Education Series, 34*(5), 375-396

Miller, B.D., Blau, G. M, Christopher, O. T. & Jordan, P. E. (2012). Sustaining and expanding systems of care to provide mental health services for children, youth and families across America. *American Journal of Community Psychology, 49*(3-4), 566- 579.

Munson, M. R., Floersch, J. E. & Townsend, L. (2009). Attitudes toward mental health services and illness perceptions among adolescents with mood disorders. *Child Adolescence and Social Work Journal, 26*, 447-466

Rahman, S. (2013). Teenage issues and ways to deal with them. *Indian Journal of Health and Wellbeing, 4*(5), 1234-1238

Samargia, L. A., Saewyc, E. M., & Elliott, B. A. (2006). Forgone mental health care and self-reported access barriers among adolescents. *The Journal of School Nursing, 22*(1), 17-26

Stadler, C., Feifel, J., Rohrmann, S., Vermeiren, R. & Poustka, F. (2010). Peer-victimization and mental health problems in adolescents: Are parental and school support protective? *Child Psychiatry and Human Development, 41*, 371-386.

United States Department of Labor (n. d.). Occupational Safety & Work Administration (OSHA). OSHA Fact Sheet: Young workers. Retrieved from *https://www.osha.gov/Publications/young_worke rs.html*

WorkSafeBC (2015). Statistics for Young workers. Retrieved from *https://www2.worksafebc.com/topics/youngwork er/Statistics.asp*

OBESITY: WHY SUCH A CONCERN FOR YOUTHS

Obesity is a major concern for young people today for several reasons, but the most important may be the fact that the predicted trend towards greater overweight and obesity will continue, and that doing nothing would aggravate the situation. This means that young people today in North America and many of the other western countries need to take stock and take action to maintain a healthy body weight.

A GLOBAL EPIDEMIC

Obesity has reached epidemic proportions globally and its incidence has doubled since 1980, "with 1.4 billion adults identified as overweight and more than 10% of the world's adult population being obese (Karp & Gesell, 2015, p. 1).

OBESITY IN THE UNITED STATES

Obesity in the United States is just as startling, with 68.5% of adults being overweight, and with 34.9% of these being obese. According to research, 31.8% of those between the ages of 2 and 19 are overweight, with 16.9% of these being obese (Karp & Gesell, 2015). The United States National Health and Nutrition Examination Survey from 2009 to 2010 showed that 12.1% of children between ages 2 and 5 "met the obesity criteria", with "26.7% of 2- to 5-year-olds (being) . . . overweight", which was up from 21.2% for this age group between 2007 and 2008 (Saavedra, et al., 2003, p. 28).

OBESITY IN CANADA

In Canada, the figures for obesity are also quite high. The Canadian Health Measures Survey which assessed the trends between 2009 and 2011 showed that 30% of adolescents were overweight or obese, with this figure having doubled since 1978. In 2011 in this country, among 12- to 17-year olds, 24% of boys and 17% of girls were overweight or obese. Also, 40% of men and 27% of women were overweight, with 20% of men and 17% of women being obese (Employment and Social Development Canada, 2016). It is further estimated by the Childhood Obesity Foundation that 70% of adults would be overweight or obese by 2040, if present trends continue.

OVERWEIGHT TRENDING FIRST YEAR UNIVERSITY

Obesity is seen as having a tremendous impact on health and so is a concern of many young people. But according to many reports, college and university students put on about 15 pounds in their freshman year.

SOME COMMONLY ACCEPTED CAUSES OF OBESITY:

EATING A MAJOR CULPRIT

This may be primarily because of eating fast foods and not engaging in regular exercise. Nutrition is also implicated. We have only to look at the most popular fast foods that young people enjoy and eat on a regular basis. These include a high level of fat, a large number of calories, and very little food value. Consequently, many young people are malnourished in a land that has an abundance of good food.

Whereas in the past, most parents ensured their children ate healthy meals and engaged in adequate physical activity, today, most parents are hard-pressed to monitor everything their children consume. The easy availability of fast foods and the fact that most young people have their own money make it increasingly difficult for parents to ensure that their children eat only healthy foods.

LACK OF PHYSICAL ACTIVITY: ANOTHER CULPRIT

Physical activity is also down with the prevalence of electronic gadgets that make it very easy for society to become even more sedentary. Children and young people, for example, sit for hours after school watching TV, video gaming, or surfing the web. The result of this lifestyle is that they miss out on good nutrition and receive little physical activity. Overweight and obesity have become common phenomena among our young people.

REAL CAUSES OF OBESITY

Although eating the wrong kinds of foods is often cited as a major cause of obesity, a question that is often not asked is why people eat the wrong kinds of food. Some of the explanations are that many people eat the wrong kinds of food because they do not have the right information about the nature of the foods they eat, they are enticed to eat the wrong foods through advertising, they do not have the time to prepare meals, and they may not be able to afford the right kinds of foods.

SOME IMPACTS OF OBESITY

Some may argue that the extra pounds that many children have are only "baby fat" that the children would outgrow as they become teenagers. Unfortunately, many fat children become fat young people and their overweight and obesity last into adulthood. Apart from malnutrition, there are other dangers such as fats that clog arteries, and food additives that have been implicated in allergies and in learning difficulties. Salt and sugar have also been implicated in high blood pressure, stroke and heart disease.

NOT HAVING THE RIGHT INFORMATION

A vast amount of information is available on the right kinds of foods to eat, but many people do not know why these foods that are recommended as good foods are really good. For example, they are told that they should eat more fruits and vegetables and some people add an apple or a spoonful of peas and carrots beside the large helpings of French fries, mashed potatoes or a good helping of rice that they have. What they often do not know is that they should have many more and different kinds of fruits and many more vegetables, and far less meat than they are used to eating. They also do not know that substituting juice for the real fruit can be counter-productive, considering that most juices have too much sugar added to be considered healthy. For example, as pointed out, the problem is that "even a single glass of orange juice can put you over the daily sugar limit recommended by the World Health Organization" (Vogel, 2015, p. E256).

BEING ENTICED TO EAT THE WRONG FOODS – ADVERTISING

Advertising is important in providing us with information about new products and services that are available. However, in the case of food advertising, some food manufacturers make enticing presentations and claims that cause us to gravitate towards getting some of these foods. What seems to capture our attention and our taste buds are the high sugar and salt content, with fatty foods being tastier than other foods. If manufacturers were to acknowledge and take responsibility for the ill effects of high fat, sugar and salt content, and reduce these substantially in their foods, then we would have a healthier society. But with the fear of reducing their share of the fast food/junk food markets, most manufacturers continue, business as usual. This means that we must use the knowledge we have and that is available to make good choices about the right foods for us and for our families.

FIND IT CONVENIENT TO BUY FAST FOODS

It is true that many people find it necessary from time to time to eat out, and many opt for the fast food restaurants. Most of the fare offered includes high levels of fat, sugar and salt in order to keep customers coming back for the tasty foods. In more recent years, health-conscious consumers have been having an impact on these restaurants that are increasingly adding healthier choices to their menus. Individuals who find it necessary to eat out can choose the healthier meals and so avoid some of the high fat, high sugar and salt content of popular fast foods. Some people are already doing that. Even so, consumers must be ever vigilant as to what manufacturers are telling them which foods are healthy.

POSSIBLE SOLUTIONS

Efforts can be made to help establish good eating habits in infants. As one source points out, "The first 2 years of life are a critical time period where parents can and should intervene to establish healthy patterns that may well last a lifetime and could help curb the obesity trend" (Saavedra et al., 2013, p. 27). This is important, considering that studies have shown that some children as young as 2 years old show signs of obesity.

Making the best food choices at all times and bearing in mind the importance of fruits and vegetables as integral parts of your diet, and not using them merely as add-ons are good pieces of advice. Remember, sometimes substitutes for fruits and vegetables could end up having added salt, sugar and fats that are harmful to health.

Reduction in the amount eaten, reduction in the amount of fast food consumed, and increased physical activity have been said to reduce the risk of developing heart disease, cancer, osteoporosis and diabetes.

As a young person heading back to school, think about these statistics. Poor nutrition and lack of exercise inevitably lead to disease and death. This may be difficult for you to understand at this time, but it is something you may want to ponder. Watch what you eat. If you have to eat at fast food outlets sometimes, choose the least damaging foods, or the foods with the least fat and calories.

CHOOSE FOODS WISELY AND EXERCISE

Cut down on foods and beverages with high salt and sugar content. School cafeterias have been accused of carrying foods that are unhealthy, namely, high in caloric value and low in nutritional value. Therefore, choose your foods wisely, and plan to include some physical activity. You could be making a decision of a lifetime, since you could reduce your chances of getting serious disease.

ARE FOODS UNAFFORDABLE?

If you find that you cannot afford buying the kinds of foods that you should eat, don't give up. There are different methods that people have been using to gain access to healthy foods. Some of these methods include being part of community gardens, food pantries, or cooperatives where groups of people buy their food in bulk from farmers and are able to pay lower prices. There are also situations where farmers are unable to harvest all their crops and where they allow consumers to pick the harvest for a fraction of the price at which those fruits and vegetables could be bought at the supermarkets. In other words, look for situations where you could go to the farm and pick your own food, thereby saving the farmer the cost of harvesting the crops, while obtaining your food at a lower price.

Maybe a Business Opportunity for You

If you are an enterprising young person, you may even find this a money-making opportunity, where you could get fruits and vegetables to the final consumer at a lower cost, by obtaining the crops directly from the farm and getting them to your neighbors, old and young alike, who either do not have the transportation, the time or the opportunity to get these for themselves. If you do, you will be providing an income for yourself, providing much needed healthy food to your neighbors, and also helping them to keep down their food bills. By being reasonable with the prices you charge and not trying to make the same profits as the supermarkets, you may find that you have a lucrative business within a few short months. Depending on where you live, consider the necessary licenses you would have to do this.

Eating more fruits and vegetables is also seen as an important way of providing the right nutrients to the body, and adopting new ways of incorporating these into a diet could also lead to weight loss.

CHAPTER 27 - REFERENCES AND FURTHER READING

Bryant, P. H., Hess, A., & Bowen, P. G. (2015). Social determinants of health related to Obesity. *The Journal for Nurse Practitioners, 11*(2), 220-226.

Employment and Social Development Canada (2016). Indicators of well-being in Canada. Health – Obesity. Retrieved from *http://well-being.esdc.gc.ca/misme-iowb/.3ndic.1t.4r@-eng.jsp?iid=6*

A Joint Report from the Public Health Agency of Canada and Canadian Institute of Heath Information (2011). Retrieved from *https://secure.cihi.ca/free_products/Obesity_in_canada_2011_en.pdf*

Karp, S. M. & Gesell, S. B. (2015). Obesity prevention and treatment in school-aged children, adolescents, and young adults - where we go from here? *Primary Prevention Insights, 5*, 1 – 4.

Saavedra, J. M., Deming, D., Dattilo, A. & Reidy, K. (2013). Lessons from the feeding infants and toddlers study in North America: What children eat, and implications for obesity prevention. *Annals of Nutrition and Metabolism, 62*(suppl 3), 27-36

Sand, A., Emaous, N. & Lian, O. (2015). Overweight and obesity in young adult women: a matter of health or appearance? The Tromso study: Fit futures. *International Journal of Qualitative Studies on Health and Well-being, 10*, 1 -12.

Shankardass, K., Lofters, A. & Kirst, M. (2002). Public awareness of income-related health inequalities in Ontario, Canada. *International Journal for Equity in Health, 11,* 26-35.

Singh, G. P., Slahpush, M. & Kogan, M. D. (2010). Neighborhood socioeconomic conditions, built environments, and childhood obesity. *Health Affairs, 29*(3), 503-512.

Vogel, L. (2015). Food guide under fire at obesity summit. *Canadian Medical Association Journal, 187*(9), E256

Young, L. R. (2002). The contribution of expanding portion sizes to the U.S. obesity epidemic. *American Journal of Public Health, 92*(2), 246-249

CHAPTER 28

SO YOU ARE TERRIFIED OF BEING FAT?

YOUNG PEOPLE AND ANOREXIA

The messages we hear from family members, friends, and the media, all tell us that we should not be fat. While some of these messages are motivated by health concerns, most of these messages are influenced by fashion, and are directed at people who are healthy, but who lack the fashionable thinness that is often associated with conceptions of beauty. Body image features vary widely in many areas, with people being judged on the basis of what their bodies look like.

PREOCCUPATION WITH BODY IMAGE AND OTHER FACTORS

Some believe that it is our preoccupation with body image that leads to anorexia nervosa and bulimia, although it is often pointed out that there are many deep-seated problems that lead to eating disorders.

ANOREXIA

Anorexia (nervosa) is the morbid fear of being fat, and is often accompanied by extreme weight loss, low self-esteem, and distorted body image. Individuals suffering from this condition see themselves as being fat, even when their bodies are emaciated. Anorexia has the highest mortality rate of any of these disorders, with half of the deaths including suicide and cardiac arrhythmia.

BULIMIA

Bulimia is the condition where individuals are preoccupied with emptying their stomachs, after having gorged themselves on a bountiful supply of food, or sometimes even after a morsel. Usually involving binge eating, bulimia is characterized by the use laxatives, diuretics, enemas, excessive exercising, stimulants such as diet pills, amphetamines, and/or intense dieting in order to get rid of the food consumed. Some people with eating disorders exhibit both anorexic and bulimic tendencies.

Bulimia is the most common of the eating disorders and is sometimes not as noticeable, since there is often very little weight loss in the case of bulimia, while in anorexia, it is most noticeable.

WHO IS AFFECTED BY EATING DISORDERS?

Both men and women could have these conditions, but it is more commonly women who suffer from anorexia and bulimia. Research has shown that over the years about 95 per cent of all anorexics were women. However, in recent years, more men are exhibiting the condition.

The onset of eating disorders is usually adolescence, about age 15, with 0.9 per cent of females and 0.5 per cent of males being affected. Women who are involved in activities where size matters are often afflicted by these conditions. Female athletes, particularly gymnasts, tennis players, models, and those involved in the fashion, television and travel industries, show a high propensity to having eating disorders.

SYMPTOMS OF ANOREXIA

What are some of the symptoms of anorexia nervosa? Some of the symptoms are excessive weight loss; hair, nail and skin problems; ceasing of menstruation; extreme sensitivity to cold temperatures; body hair growth; edema or swelling around the ankles; unusual eating habits; preoccupation with food, weight or calories; weighing often; extreme physical activity; social isolation; poor self-esteem; wearing large clothes; and denial of having a problem. Any number of these symptoms could be cause for concern. If you manifest a number of these symptoms, maybe it is time to admit that you may have a problem and do something about it before it is too late. A good place to start is with your family doctor.

MEDIA AGGRAVATE THE SITUATION

From listening to various experts, we could conclude that while the media do not cause eating disorders, they may be responsible for pushing those who have the condition or who have the susceptibility to the condition to become more seriously preoccupied with their body image. However, most psychologists and those involved with eating disorders contend that eating disorders have a much deeper root than media presentation of female body image. Some point out that it is all about control.

EXPERIENCES OF DEALING WITH EATING DISORDERS

One young woman who was afflicted with anorexia pointed out that there were other problems in her life, and that being preoccupied with food took her mind away from these other problems. Having to count calories and think about food were activities that she found less painful than dealing with her problems. Many anorexics point out that they substitute concern over food and calories for problems such as lack of assertiveness and fear of failure and disappointment. Others point out that it is in the area of food that they have control.

SOCIAL CAUSES FOR EATING DISORDERS

While some people believe that psychological and psychiatric problems, as well as chemical imbalance, are the causes of anorexia and bulimia, others look for social causes. Rigid family life, family dysfunction, and social problems, including child sexual abuse, are also seen as factors contributing to eating disorders. In some instances, even after anorexics are diagnosed, the seat of their problem remains uncovered. Since bulimics are often not identified for years, their eating problems often go untreated. Therefore, eating disorders pose a very serious threat to physical and mental health and to the lives of those afflicted with the disorders.

NOTE THE DANGER SIGNS FOR EATING DISORDERS

Therefore, as a young person, note the danger signs associated with eating disorders. Make sure that your concern with losing weight and dieting does not move into the unhealthy range. If you suspect that you may be having such a problem, seek counselling right away. Start with your family doctor who could help you identify your condition. If you are afraid that a friend or loved one may be afflicted with an eating disorder, speak to that person about the possibility that this is the case, and support and encourage him or her to seek help and undertake a treatment protocol. It is likely that person may be upset with you for thinking so, but in the long run that person would see that it is out of concern that you broached the subject.

PROFESSIONAL HELP STRONGLY RECOMMENDED

Individuals who believe that they may have an eating disorder are encouraged to seek treatment immediately. However, it is important to do the research, looking at the support systems that clinics have to offer. Make sure that a clinic meets your needs or the needs of your loved ones that have the condition. Having the support of family and friends is vital to dealing with these disorders.

HOW YOU CAN HELP

Several experts recommend that as a friend, family member, teacher, athletic coach or trainer, or someone dealing with young people, you could play an important part in allaying fears about body image and in identifying when the young people around you or in your care are becoming preoccupied with food and dieting. Where it is apparent that your family member or friend may have an eating disorder, you can help by encouraging that person to speak to his or her parents and getting professional help. You can also help by not aggravating the situation, and by not teasing your family member or friend about weight issues, even as a joke. Encourage participation in athletic activities and exercise for healthy living, but discourage excessive exercising. Depending on your relationship, you can become an exercise buddy for your family member or friend, thereby helping your family member or friend not to go overboard in their exercising. Eating disorders are a serious problem, requiring professional help as soon as possible.

CHAPTER 28 - REFERENCES AND FURTHER READING

Boschi, V., Siervo, M., D'Orsi, P., Margiotta, N., Trapanese, E. et al. (2003). Body composition, eating behavior, food-body concerns and eating disorders in adolescent girls. *Annals of Nutrition & Metabolism, 47*(6), 284-293.

Currie, Al (2010). Sport and eating disorders – Understanding and managing the risks. *Asian Journal of Sports Medicine, 1*(2), 63-68

Redston, S., Tiller, J., Schweitzer, I., Keks, N., Burrows, G. et al. (2014). 'Help us, she's fading away': How to manage the patient with anorexia nervosa. *Australian Family Physician, 43*(8), 531-536.

Robertson, L. & Thomson, D. (2014). Giving permission to be fat? Examining the impact of body-based belief systems. *Canadian Journal of Education, 37*(4), 1-25.

Stelter, R. (2015). 'I tried so many diets, now I want to do it differently: A single case study on coaching for weight loss. *International Journal of Qualitative studies on Health & Well-being,* 1-14.

CHAPTER 29

SO YOU WANT TO BULK UP?

CAUTION ABOUT STEROIDS & SYNTHENTIC HGH ABUSE

You are a young man. You want to look like the pictures you see in the magazines, but you believe you can't. Maybe you think you are too skinny, and your muscles are too small. You worry that your chest is not well-developed. You hate your arms and hands, because you think they have grown too long, and all in all you feel that you do not look right. To make matters worse, you have a bad case of acne. You are becoming more and more concerned. Would you ever change? Six months have gone by and you have only grown taller and skinnier. Some of your classmates call you names and you wish things could change.

Is There a Solution?

Well, you met Jon last night. He used to be like you, and then you hadn't seen him for a while. There he is now, muscles and all. Jon has really bulked up. You asked him what exercises he was doing at the gym, and he told you, and then he confessed that he was also using some tablets as well as capsules, which he got from a good friend. You realized that he could be using steroids or some performance-enhancing drug. Jon tried to convince you that what he was taking was quite safe; if not, he would not be using it.

He told you it was not steroids, but just something to help your body develop. You start feeling excited about the prospect of you looking like Jon.

YOU FEEL YOU HAVE A CHOICE

You see this as an opportunity to make changes. You have been thinking: you could stay as you are and hope for the best, you could exercise and maybe it would help, or you could take the capsules or tablets, and hope that you could look like Jon. You had been dreaming about changes, and now as you have seen Jon, you believe there is a possibility for you.

NOT A GOOD IDEA

You tell your friend, Teddy, about your discovery. After all, Teddy is your best friend and both of you do everything together. But Teddy does not think it is a good idea, because he had read an article some time ago about steroids and synthetic human growth hormone (HGH). He knows that steroids could come in the form of tablets, capsules, and even in the form of a gel, and that HGH comes in pill form as well as in injection. Teddy tells you that it is either of these drugs, and that it is not a good idea. He is not going to try it. You are really disappointed, but Teddy is a smart boy. That is what everybody says about Teddy.

You eventually call Jon and tell him that you are not going to try out his supplement just yet. You want to find out more information what he is taking. But Jon tries to assure you there is nothing really to find out about. All the guys at his gym are using the same thing, and they are fine. You ask Jon what it is and he cannot give you a name, except to say that it is a supplement in the form of tablets. You are tempted. You reason that Teddy does not have a problem with his appearance, as you do. Maybe if Teddy was as skinny as you are, maybe he would try it. What if you are wrong in not taking up Jon on his offer, and you miss out on the one thing that would help you improve your appearance?

Anyway, you decide to do some research on your own. You tell yourself, even if it is steroids or HGH (whatever that is), if it doesn't kill you, you will take it. You want to read up on it before you use it. You recall how one of your friends, Hank, was trying out something he got over the Internet, and died as a result of an overdose. You don't want to be like him. You decide to find out more about steroids and HGH on your own before you do anything. Wise Decision!!

After some digging, this is some of what you have found out on your own.

STEROID & HGH USE AMONG YOUTHS

Although weightlifters, some athletes, and bodybuilders, use steroids and HGH for performance enhancement, many ordinary young people use these drugs to develop their bodies and improve their appearance. Whereas it was once thought that it was only males that used these drugs, today females are increasingly using these drugs, with male and female teens using HGH at a proportion of 12% to 9% (Beckham, 2014). A national report revealed that in 2013 11% of teenagers reported that they had used HGH at least once, and this use was up from 5% in 2012 (Feliz, 2013). Another source reported: "Steroid use among teens has increased from 5 per cent in 2009 to 7 per cent in 2013. But the latest percentage of HGH use is more than double the previous year" (Beckham, 2014).

However, according to one source, "Recent surveys indicate that the prevalence of androgen (steroid) use among adolescents has decreased over the past 10-15 years" (Hoffman, Kraemer, Bhasin, Storer, Ratamess, Haff, Willoughby & Rogol, 2009, p. S1). Since these researchers are working with young athletes, these findings show that young athletes are less likely to be involved in using steroids than they were at one time. Kanayama and Pope (2012) point out that it is a misconception that steroids are abused primarily by athletes, and that these drugs have found their way into the mainstream society where they are used more by regular individuals and not athletes.

WHAT ARE STEROIDS?

They are synthetic substances that mimic the actions of male sex hormones in the body. They help promote the growth of muscles and the development of male characteristics. They also reduce body fat. Young men who want to improve their physical appearance, as well as males and females who want to improve their performance, often see steroids as something that could help them. Many young people find steroids easy to use since steroids can be taken in tablet or capsule form, can be injected and can even be rubbed on the skin as a cream. This is only part of the story. See the rest of the story below.

WHAT IS HGH?

HGH is a natural hormone that is produced by the pituitary gland and which is seen as spurring on growth in children and adolescents. However, the synthetic production of this hormone which was produced in 1985 has been used to treat certain diseases. But its abuse for improving body image has increased, without many people realizing that there are serious side effects that are associated with its illegal use. Some contend that it is still too early to realize all the side effects that could result from the abuse of these substances.

SOME KNOWN PHYSICAL AND PSYCHOLOGICAL SIDE EFFECTS

Steroids are very appealing, but highly damaging. Steroid use has increased over the years as there is a great deal of emphasis on body image. While for women, body image is one of thinness, for men, body image is one of having a hard and muscular body. A similar comment could be made about the appeal to use HGH. However, research has shown that the use of these drugs can be detrimental to health.

STEROIDS AND SHRINKING OF MALE SEX ORGANS

Steroids have been said to increase the female hormone, estrogen, which can have the serious side effect in men, for example, of causing men to start developing breasts. More than that, steroid use was also associated with disruptions in hormones, which could lead to baldness, painful erections, shrinkage of testicles, and loss of function of these male sex organs (U.S. Department of Justice). Some physical effects include fluid retention, yellowing of the skin, and increase in bad cholesterol levels (U.S. Department of Justice). Decrease in the good cholesterol in the body is also associated with increased risk of heart disease and liver disease (U.S. Department of Justice).

STEROIDS AND REDUCTION OF BREASTS AND MORE IN FEMALES

For females, steroid use could lead to the growth of facial and body hair, deepened voice, breast reduction, enlarged clitoris, and menstrual irregularities (U.S. Department of Justice). The same negative physical effects found in males also appear in females who use steroids, including risk of heart and liver disease.

PSYCHOLOGICAL EFFECTS OF STEROID USE

Both males and females also share in some of the psychological side effects, including mood swings, increased hostility and aggressiveness.

PHYSICAL AND PSYCHOLOGICAL SIDE EFFECTS OF HGH USE

Use of HGH also has some side effects which include pain in the nerves, muscles and joints, swelling due to fluid retention, numbness and tingling of the skin, and increase the risk of diabetes and the growth of cancerous tumors (Ratini, 2014). Because these drugs are obtained illegally or from unregulated sources, there is also no guarantee as to their safety.

ILLEGAL ACTIVITY WITH STIFF PENALTIES

Besides these negative physical and psychological side effects, there are legal consequences. There is widespread abuse of anabolic steroids by individuals who obtain these drugs illegally, but there are harsh penalties related to possession and sale of these drugs. As the U.S. Department of Justice observed: "The possession or sale of anabolic steroids without a valid prescription is illegal.

Simple possession of illicitly obtained anabolic steroids carries a maximum penalty of one year in prison and a minimum $1,000 fine if this is an individual's first drug offense. The maximum penalty for trafficking is five years in prison and a fine of $250,000 if this is the individual's first felony drug offense." The penalties become even more severe, if the individual is a habitual offender.

EMBARRASSMENT IN SPORTS

Steroid use is frowned upon in sports, and athletes have been disqualified from competition because they have been identified as having used steroids to improve their performance. In fact, steroid use is seen as giving an unnatural advantage to an athlete.

It is shown that athletes are the ones with great motivation to enhance their performance and some may be tempted to use performance enhancement drugs. As one source observes, "In a recent survey of 3,705 kids, 11 percent of teens in grades 9 through 12 reported having used synthetic human growth hormone without a prescription. That means that at any high school football game, it's likely that at least two players in the field will have tried human growth hormone" (Beckham, 2004). When discovered as having used performance-enhancing drugs, athletes are not only disqualified, but disgraced.

ATHLETES ENCOURAGED TO BECOME HIGHLY SKILLED

But there is an answer. Instead of resorting to these drugs, athletes are encouraged to become more highly skilled. The National Strength and Conditioning Association (NSCA) (2009) takes a stand against the use of these performance-enhancing drugs. "The NSCA rejects the use of androgens and HGH or any performance-enhancing drugs on the basis of ethics, the ideals of fair play in competition, and concerns for the athlete's health" (Hoffman et al., 2009, p. S1). It is not fair that some athletes use drugs to improve their performance when they are competing with other athletes who depend on their natural talents and skills.

The recommendation is therefore that there should be ongoing education to "help athletes, coaches, and strength and conditioning professionals become knowledgeable, highly skilled, and technically trained in their approach to exercise program design and implementation" (Hoffman et al., 2009, S5).

TOO HEAVY A PRICE TO PAY ALL AROUND

Although steroids and HGH are said to have some good effects on the body, they do not work for everyone. Even if they did work, what is the sense of having a good-looking body or being good in sports for a short time, if you won't live long enough to enjoy either of these? If you are a young person who is ungainly at the present time, who does not feel comfortable with your appearance, know that with time, your body will develop, so don't worry. This is the natural process of development, where different parts of your body will very likely develop unevenly over time. Be patient, and things will fall into place. Eat right, exercise, and rest, and let Nature do the rest! Think of the caterpillar as it changes into a butterfly and the saying by Annette Thomas: "Just when the caterpillar thought "I am incapable of moving," it became a butterfly."

After going through this information, you have come up with the right decision. It is not worth the risk to jeopardize your good health for the promise of a good-looking body and possibly poor health. Maybe there is a good-looking body in your future, just as the ugly and ungainly caterpillar will turn into a beautiful butterfly. Let Nature take its course to help you develop into the person you were meant to be.

CHAPTER 29 - REFERENCES AND FURTHER READING

Beckham, J. (2014). Growth hormone usage rises among teens. Wired. Retrieved from *http://www.deadiversion.usdoj.gov/pubs/brochures/steroids/children/*

Feliz, J. (2013). National Study: Teens report higher use of performance enhancing substances. Partnership for Drug-free kids. Retrieved from *http://www.drugfree.org/newsroom/pats-2013-teens-report-higher-use-of-performance-enhancing-substances*

Hoffman, J. R., Kraemer, W. J., Bhasin, S., Storer, T., Raramess, N. A., Haff, G. G., Willoughby, D. S., & Rogol, A. D. (2009). Position stand on androgen and human growth hormone use, *Journal of Strength and Conditioning Research, 23*(Supplement 5), S1 – S59.

Kanayama, G. & Pope, H. G. Jr. (2012)/. Misconceptions about anabolic-Androgenic steroid abuse. *Psychiatric Annals, 42*(1), 371-375.

Kindred. Dave, "Ask a tough question, get a tough answer: What can steroids do to you?" *Sporting News,* July 12, 2004, Vol. 228, Iss. 28.

Ratini, M. (2014). Human Growth Hormone (HGH). WebMD. Retrieved from *http://www.webmd.com/fitness-exercise/human-growth-hormone-hgh?page=1*

Thomas, A. Quote on Butterflies. Retrieved at *http://www.goodreads.com/quotes/tag/butterfly*

U.S. Department of Justice. Office of Diversion Control (n.d.). Steroid Use by school age children. Retrieved from *http://www.deadiversion.usdoj.gov/pubs/brochures/steroids/children/*

CHAPTER 30

TAKING RESPONSIBILITY FOR CHOOSING YOUR GOVERNMENT

Whatever governments are elected now in this second decade of the 21st century will be important, considering that these years are formative in your lives. For teens and young adults, these are the years when you are attaining your education, beginning your careers, starting your families, and laying the foundation for the rest of your lives. You need to see to it that governments that are in place are governments that would provide good governance that would benefit the whole society.

In recent months, with upcoming elections, some young people are playing a significant part in promoting candidates that they believe would make a change in areas that are in deficit. This is noteworthy as young people are looking more closely at the programs and values that make up the platforms of their respective governments. Other young people may still be on the fence and not taking sides, while others may be apathetic. These are some of the conditions that are taking place in the United States, Canada, and in many other countries.

EXPECTATIONS OF GOVERNMENT'S ROLES

It is necessary that government serves the role for which it is elected. Speaking about the three essential roles of government, Slaughter (February 13, 2017) maintains that governments should protect their citizens, should provide "a social security that enables citizens to create their own economic security" and should invest in their citizens to allow them to be able to provide for themselves. Another source shows the responsibility of government should be to provide for social justice to its citizens. This involves paying attention to human rights, equity of opportunities, social safety, poverty reduction, capacity and empowerment, and ending misuse of social justice (Office for Social Justice, 2016). Further, as another source declares, "The government, acting on behalf of the people, declares certain actions to be just and unjust" (Messmore, September 17, 2007).

As pointed out, this responsibility for providing social justice "must be undertaken by the government and then be extended down to each individual where everybody participates according to their own capacity" (Office for Social Justice, 2016). Considering government as having the roles of protecting, providing goods and services, investing in its citizens and allowing for the promotion of social justice, young people can assess whether their existing governments are meeting these expectations with respect to good governance.

BE CRITICAL THINKERS

However, the time is urgent for all young people to see the significance of having good governance in their respective countries. All young people must be encouraged to be critical thinkers. It is time that young people speak out for what they believe to be the desired values for their societies. It is not enough to simply accept what is given, particularly if that falls short of expectations.

Young people, you who are more sophisticated and who have become skilled in critical thinking, must use your abilities to effect change. Thoroughly analyze the platforms of those who present themselves as candidates. Don't be fooled by bluster, grandstanding, and generalities. Demand the details of platforms of candidates as to how they intend to get things done. It is not enough for them to say, "I will make the world a better place" or "Everyone will be better off". Demand and scrutinize the details and ask yourselves, "Are these details workable?" "In light of the present situation, can these details be achieved?" "Do the candidates know what really happens in real life or are they presenting us with wishful thinking?" "Are they realistic in their ideas or are they all bluster and hot air?" "Are they taking us further into the 21st century or are they taking us back to the 19th?" "Are they reasonable in thinking about the whole electorate or do they have the interests of only a certain privileged segment of the population at heart?" "Do they represent everyone and will they take us into an age where everyone has the opportunity to excel?"

STILL TOO YOUNG TO VOTE?

Maybe you are still too young to vote, but you are not too young to prepare yourself for this important duty. In order to make the right decisions, you need to know what is going on. Knowing what is happening on the political front and what the different political parties stand for are essential. You need to know what candidates represent and how government works. As a young person, you also need to become informed about important issues facing the society now.

MAYBE RUN FOR OFFICE IN A FEW YEARS

In a matter of years, you would be one of the people making decisions through your vote as to what should happen. You also have the potential to be one of those running for office, fully aware of what government should be, and fully and competently prepared to deliver on expectations. But without adequate information and preparation, you'd vote haphazardly or not vote at all; and you won't be ready to take your place as credible candidates for political office.

THIS IS YOUR RESPONSIBILITY

At this time in your life, you can no longer depend on your parents or older people to tell you what is good for you. As you mature, as you recognize how this new world of the 21st century is changing, you are in the position to question any false promises that are being made and to recognize that some of the programs that are being put forward cannot work: they are not feasible. At the same time, there would be ongoing programs that your parents believe in and which make sense. But check them out yourself.

You must take responsibility for deciding which political platforms are good and can work for the wellbeing of society and which you should follow. Be the ones making the decision by using your votes intelligently. Don't be pressured or fooled into accepting blind promises.

It would be a travesty for you to follow blindly, since you would be either misusing, or not using, the most powerful instrument you have in our democracies: your vote. When you know what the issues are, when you know where the political parties stand, when you know where candidates stand on issues, then you cannot be tricked into supporting a candidate who just does not represent your interests. Knowing the various positions and taking a stand, you are in a good position to discuss these with your family members. Be prepared to take a stand against family positions, if these do not pass the test of critical thinking. Have meaningful discussions with your friends, which would help you understand issues better.

Therefore, critical thinking on the roles and responsibilities of government, assessment of how well candidates and politicians perceive these roles and responsibilities and deliver on promises, and not family loyalty, should be your guide in deciding how to use your votes in upcoming elections. After all, it is your life circumstances and those of your family and community that should be now in focus.

CHAPTER 30 - FOOD FOR THOUGHT

TOPICS AND IDEAS FOR SELF-REFLECTION AND DISCUSSION

Self-Reflection

Where do I get my information about what is going on in government?

Where do I get information about political parties and candidates running for office?

Do I get this information from a variety of sources, or do I have only one source?

Am I aware when a source of information is biased?

Do I use critical thinking to make my own decisions, or do I simply follow whatever my family says?

Group Discussion

How do young people become politically active?

How do young people become critical thinkers?

Groups and classes should undertake discussions, not about candidates and their political parties, but about how government and societies work to promote democracy.

CHAPTER 30 - REFERENCES AND FURTHER READING

Messmore, R. (September 17, 2007). Government for the
Good of the People: Ten questions about freedom,
virtue, and the role of government. Heritage
Organization. Available at
https://www.heritage.org/civil-
society/report/government-the-good-the-people-
ten-questions-about-freedomvirtue-and-the-role

Office for Social Justice (2016). The Government an
ensuring social justice. Available at
http://www.osjspm.org/the-government-and-
ensuring-social-justice

Slaughter, A. (February 13, 2017). 3 responsibilities every
government has towards its citizens. World
Economic Forum. Available at
https://www.weforum.org/agenda/2017/02/govern
ment-responsibility-to-citizens-anne-marie-
slaughter/

CHAPTER 31

CONCLUSION

Now that you are at the end of this book, I hope some of the ideas expressed have reminded you of some of the responsibilities you have as an adolescent on the verge of adulthood. I also hope that you have envisaged opportunities for sharing some of these ideas with others.

If you are an older adult, I hope you gained something from this book and that you will share some of these ideas with your children, students or other young people with whom you interact on a regular basis. And remember, you can always gift a copy of this book to a younger person.

If you are a teacher, youth group leader, or another adult youth worker, you may be able to use topics in this book as prompts for discussion. Fireside or online chats, dinner conversations, and class discussions are excellent opportunities for sharing some of these ideas with others.

Thanks for taking the time to read this book. Please share with others, and if you find this book helpful, help others to find this book through your online reviews wherever you obtained this book. If you have ideas as to how to improve this book, please send feedback to info@SuccessfulYouthLiving.com.

MORE READING AVAILABLE

If you found this book beneficial, you may also consider trying out some of the other books in this series at https://SuccessfulYouthLiving.com. See below or the back of this book for details. You can also read our blog at https://SuccessfulYouthLivingBlog.com

Thanks for reading!